MW00649487

Ooey Gooey Science

Authors: SCHYRLET CAMERON and CAROLYN CRAIG

Editors: MARY DIETERICH and SARAH M. ANDERSON

Proofreader: MARGARET BROWN

COPYRIGHT © 2012 Mark Twain Media, Inc.

ISBN 978-1-58037-617-4

Printing No. CD-404164

Mark Twain Media, Inc., Publishers
Distributed by Carson-Dellosa Publishing LLC

Visit us at www.carsondellosa.com

Table of Contents

Introduction to the Teacher 1

Hands-On Activities

Matter: Oobleck 2

Non-Newtonian Fluid: Blubber 5

Weather: Making Lightning 7

Chemical Change: Polymer Bouncing Ball 9

Acids and Bases: Secret Message 11

Rocks and Minerals: Briquette Crystals 13

Physical Change: It's in the Bag Ice Cream 15

Teacher Demonstrations

Atoms: Glowing Pickle 17

Atmospheric Pressure: Bottled Egg 19

Things to Make

Light: Bubble Observatory 21

Sound: Squawking String 23

Motion: Balloon-Powered Racer 25

Friction: Air Cushion Vehicle 27

Electricity: Electronic Quiz Game 29

Bernoulli's Principle: Squeeze Bottle Rocket Launcher 31

Machines: Mousetrap Racer 33

Gravity: Egg Drop Contraption 35

Density: Pop Bottle Lava Lamp 37

Experiments

Sorbents: Oil Spill Clean-Up 39

Law of Conservation of Matter: Gas in a Bag 45

Electromagnetic Spectrum: Sunscreen 49

Evaporation: Instant Snow 53

Scoring Guide: Ooey Gooey Science Investigation Rubric 57

Answer Keys 58

Bibliography 60

National Science Standards Matrix 61

Photo Credits 62

Introduction to the Teacher

Students live in an exploding age of technology. Sometimes the volume of information can completely overwhelm students, causing them to become discouraged. *Ooey Gooey Science Investigations* is a great motivational tool that promotes science learning by stimulating student curiosity.

Motivating students is one of the fundamental challenges facing educators in science. This book focuses on providing teachers with awesome activities they can use to increase student interest and enthusiasm in learning basic science principles. Each lesson is jam-packed with illustrations and clear, step-by-step instructions to help students have fun while learning how things work and why things happen in the world around them. Doing the hands-on activities will help students explore the basic scientific ideals that play a role in their everyday lives, using ordinary items that can be found in most science classrooms or right at home. This book is ideal for teachers with limited access to a full science lab.

Ooey Gooey Science Investigations is divided into four sections. The first section focuses on fun Hands-On Activities. The second section features two Teacher Demonstrations. More advanced classes may be able to complete these activities, but due to the use of electric currents and matches, supervision of students is highly recommended. The third section, Things to Make, are exciting activities that can be done individually or in student teams. The final section, Experiments, encourages students to utilize each step of the Scientific Method to perform the experiments. Activities may also be done as whole-class experiments, demonstrations, or projects. Choice of method will depend on lab facilities, availability of equipment and supplies, time, and learning styles of students.

Ooey Gooey Science Investigations is designed to:

- **Engage students**: Students learn scientific knowledge and understanding by doing science.

- **Promote inquiry**: The Scientific Method is stressed as students explore topics related to earth science, physical science, and life science.

- **Provide real-world connections**: Topics relating to earth science, physical science, and life science are relevant to students' lives.

- **Facilitate learning styles**: The book supports planning for the diverse learning styles and skill levels of middle-school students. The easy-to-read, easy-to-follow format of the student pages will not overwhelm the struggling science student.

Ooey Gooey Science Investigations supports the STEM initiative. The hands-on activities are designed to strengthen scientific literacy. The book promotes student knowledge and understanding of science concepts through the use of good scientific techniques. The content supports the National Science Education Standards (NSES) and the National Common Core State Standards developed under the leadership of the National Governors' Association Center for Best Practices and the Council of Chief State School Officers. For correlations to state, national, and provincial standards, visit www.carsondellosa.com.

Matter: Oobleck
Background Information

Classroom Ideas

Oobleck is a hands-on activity that can be used to introduce, demonstrate, or reinforce concepts relating to the following topics:

Topics	How the Activity Relates to the Topic
States of Matter	Sometimes oobleck behaves like a solid and other times like a liquid. Oobleck feels like a liquid when it is being mixed. When the surface is tapped with a spoon, it feels like a solid. Place a scoop of oobleck in your hand. When squeezed, it forms a solid. Stop squeezing and it will run like a liquid. What causes the oobleck to act like a solid or like a liquid? Pressure. When enough pressure is applied, the oobleck acts like a solid. When little or no pressure is applied, it acts like a liquid. Oobleck is made up of long chains of molecules. If you press hard and fast, they get so tangled up that the oobleck can't move. If you press on the oobleck slowly, the chains have time to move.
Physical Change	Oobleck is an example of a physical change. When water and cornstarch are mixed, no new substance is formed. The cornstarch is suspended in the water. When the water evaporates from the mixture, the cornstarch will be left behind.
Suspensions	Oobleck is made up of tiny, solid particles of cornstarch suspended in water. Cornstarch and water is a colloidal suspension. A colloidal suspension is one in which the starch and water are not dissolved but simply mixed into a permanent suspension that will not settle on standing.
Viscosity	The viscosity or resistance to flow of oobleck changes. Run your finger through a bowl of water; the water moves out of the way. Try running your finger through a bowl of oobleck. The oobleck resists. Pick up a handful of oobleck; it flows.
Non-Newtonian Fluid	Oobleck is called a non-Newtonian fluid. It does not follow the rules of liquids that Newton discovered. A non-Newtonian fluid has properties of both a solid and a liquid and reacts to stress with increased viscosity. If you press a finger on the surface of a non-Newtonian fluid, the stress introduced by the incoming force causes the atoms in the fluid to rearrange such that it behaves like a solid. Your finger will not go through. If you shove your finger into the fluid slowly, however, it will penetrate successfully. If you pull your finger out abruptly, it will again behave like a solid.
Polymer	Cornstarch is a polymer found in nature. It comes from corn. Cornstarch is made up of long chains of molecules. Adding a polymer to a liquid makes it harder for the liquid to move or increases its reaction time. If you press hard and fast, the chains of molecules get so tangled up that the oobleck can't move. If you press on the oobleck slowly, the chains have time to move.

Related Vocabulary

- **chemical change**: a reaction that transforms a substance into a new substance with different properties
- **colloidal suspension**: a mixture in a continuous liquid phase in which the solid is suspended in the liquid
- **fluid**: any state of matter that can flow with relative ease: gas, liquid, plasma
- **gas**: a substance that has no definite shape or volume
- **liquid**: a substance with a definite volume but no definite shape
- **matter**: the term used to describe anything that has mass and takes up space
- **mixture**: a substance consisting of two or more substances mixed together
- **monomer**: a simple compound whose molecules can join together to form polymers
- **non-Newtonian fluid**: a fluid whose flow properties do not follow the rules that Newton discovered most liquids follow
- **physical change**: a change from one state (solid or liquid or gas) to another without a change in chemical composition
- **plasma**: a substance with no definite shape or volume that is a highly energized gas
- **polymer**: a naturally occurring or synthetic compound consisting of large molecules made up of a linked series of repeated simple monomers
- **solid**: a substance with a definite volume and a definite shape
- **states of matter**: the physical forms in which a substance can exist: solid, liquid, gas, and plasma
- **suspension**: a mixture in which fine particles are suspended in a fluid where they are supported by buoyancy
- **viscosity**: the property of resistance to flow in a fluid

Real-World Connection

Paint is an example of a non-Newtonian fluid. Paint adheres to a brush when at rest but glides on easily when the brush is applied to a surface. Quicksand is a dangerous non-Newtonian fluid. Ketchup is a non-Newtonian fluid that we eat on our French fries. The best way to get ketchup to flow is to turn the bottle over and be patient. Tapping the bottom of the bottle actually slows the ketchup down!

Name: _____ Date: _____

Oobleck

Purpose: Discover the properties of oobleck

Materials

newspaper   graduated cylinder or measuring cup
cornstarch   large bowl
food coloring   water
triple-beam balance scale

Procedure

Step #1: Cover the work area with newspaper.

Step #2: Place 750 g (1 1/2 cups) of cornstarch in the bowl.

Step #3: Add two drops of food coloring to 500 mL (1 cup) of water. Add water to the bowl slowly, mixing the cornstarch and water with your fingers until all the powder is wet. Keep adding water until the oobleck feels like a liquid when you are mixing it slowly. Then try tapping on the surface with your finger or a spoon. When oobleck is just right, it won't splash—it will feel solid.

Step #4: If the oobleck is too powdery, add a little more water. If it's too thin, add more cornstarch.

Step #5: Pick up a handful of oobleck and squeeze. Stop squeezing and open your hand. Rest your fingers on the surface of the oobleck. Let them sink down to the bottom of the bowl. Then try to pull them out fast. Record your observations.

Observations

_____

_____

_____

_____

Conclusion

Why does the oobleck behave like a liquid sometimes and a solid other times?

_____

_____

_____

_____

Non-Newtonian Fluid: Blubber
Background Information

Classroom Ideas

Blubber is a hands-on activity that can be used to introduce, demonstrate, or reinforce concepts relating to the following topics:

Topics	How the Activity Relates to the Topic
Non-Newtonian Fluid	Blubber is called a non-Newtonian fluid. It does not follow the rules of liquids that Newton discovered. A non-Newtonian fluid has properties of both a solid and a liquid and reacts to stress with increased viscosity. Most fluids have less viscosity the more you manipulate them. For example, when honey warms up, it runs faster. Therefore, it is a Newtonian fluid. Non-Newtonian fluids do just the opposite. They get more solid when they are manipulated. If you let your blubber sit on a surface, it pools out into an icky flowing mess. Playing with your blubber makes it thicker.
Polymer	A polymer is a naturally occurring or synthetic compound consisting of large molecules made up of a linked series of repeated simple monomers. The glue mixture is the polymer. When mixed with the cross-linking borax solution, the polymer chains become harder, forming "stretchy chains" that we call blubber.

Related Vocabulary

- **matter**: the term used to describe anything that has mass and takes up space
- **mixture**: a substance consisting of two or more substances mixed together
- **molecule**: the smallest part of a compound that still has the properties of the compound
- **monomer**: a simple compound whose molecules can join together to form polymers
- **non-Newtonian fluid**: a fluid whose flow properties do not follow the rules that Newton discovered most liquids follow
- **physical change**: a change from one state (solid or liquid or gas) to another without a change in chemical composition
- **polymer**: a naturally occurring or synthetic compound consisting of large molecules made up of a linked series of repeated simple monomers
- **solution**: a mixture in which the particles are too small to see
- **states of matter**: the physical forms in which a substance can exist: solid, liquid, gas, and plasma
- **viscosity**: the property of resistance to flow in a liquid

Real-World Connection

In 1939, nylon was invented. This synthetic polymer was spun into fiber and woven into fabrics to make clothing. It was also used to make parachutes in World War II. Another strong synthetic polymer is Kevlar. It is strong enough to stop bullets!

Name: _____ Date: _____

Blubber

Purpose: Explore the properties of a non-Newtonian fluid

Materials

glue	food coloring
bowl	plastic cup
wooden spoon	resealable baggie
borax	graduated cylinder or measuring cup
water	mL measuring spoon

Procedure

Step #1: Thoroughly mix 125 mL (1/2 cup) of glue with 125 mL (1/2 cup) of water in the bowl.

Step #2: Add 3 to 4 drops of your favorite color of food coloring to the glue/water mixture and set aside.

Step #3: In the plastic cup, mix 2.5 mL (1/2 teaspoon) of borax with 125 mL (1/2 cup) of water until dissolved.

Step #4: Add the borax solution to the glue mixture. Stir quickly with the wooden spoon.

Step #5: Pour the blubber into your hands and begin pulling and stretching the mixture.

Step #6: Store your blubber in a resealable baggie when you are not using it.

Caution: Never eat any of the materials used to make blubber.

Observations

_____

_____

_____

_____

Conclusion

_____

_____

_____

_____

Try

The molecules in your blubber become entangled the more you play with it. This makes it firmer. Adding more borax solution to your blubber will also firm its consistency. If you let your blubber sit, it will loosen its bonds and ooze more like liquid.

Weather: Making Lightning
Background Information

Classroom Ideas

Making Lightning is a hands-on activity that can be used to introduce, demonstrate, or reinforce concepts relating to the following topics:

Topics	How the Activity Relates to the Topic
Static Electricity	Static electricity is electricity at rest. Lightning is a discharge of static electricity. It represents nature's most powerful display of static electricity. This activity demonstrates that lightning is a discharge of static electricity.
Atoms	Understanding the basics of an atom helps us see how lightning is formed. Lightning happens because of the attraction between opposite charges. Protons and electrons of an atom carry an electrical charge. Protons carry a "positive" charge, while electrons carry a "negative" charge. Objects with opposite charges attract each other. Lightning happens when electrons in the bottom of a cloud are attracted to protons in the ground.

Related Vocabulary

- **atom**: the smallest part of an element; an atom is made up of electrons, protons, and neutrons
- **electricity**: the interaction between electric charges
- **electron**: an invisible, negatively charged particle that travels around the nucleus of an atom
- **lightning**: powerful discharge of static electricity
- **neutron**: an uncharged particle located in the nucleus of an atom
- **nucleus**: the positively charged, central part of an atom
- **proton**: a positively charged particle in the nucleus of an atom
- **static electricity**: a buildup of charges on an object

Real-World Connection

It is important to understand lightning since it can strike almost anywhere. Scientists estimate that lightning hits somewhere on the earth about 100 times every second. Lightning is deadly. Between 60 and 100 Americans die each year from lightning strikes. Many others are struck and survive, but often they suffer health problems as a result.

Lightning can strike as far as 10 miles away from a storm. Therefore, the safest place to be is in your home away from windows and water. You can tell how far away lightning has struck by counting the seconds between the flash and the thunder. Every 5 seconds roughly equals one mile, so if you count 5 seconds until you hear the thunder, the lightning flash was 1 mile away.

Name: _____ Date: _____

Making Lightning

Purpose: Observe how lightning forms

Materials

Styrofoam plate
thumbtack
new pencil
(or Styrofoam cup and tape)
aluminum pie pan
piece of wool fabric

Procedure

Step #1: Punch the thumbtack through the center of the aluminum pie pan from the bottom.

Step #2: Place the eraser end of the pencil on the thumbtack. The pencil will be the handle to lift the pan. You can also tape a Styrofoam cup to the center of the pie pan as shown in the photo above.

Step #3: Put the Styrofoam plate upside-down on a table. Rub the bottom hard and fast with the piece of wool for one minute.

Step #4: Using the pencil handle, pick up the pie pan and place it on top of the Styrofoam plate.

Step #5: Now, touch the pie pan with your finger. If nothing happens, try rubbing the plate again.

Observations

_____

_____

_____

_____

Conclusion

How does this experiment relate to the formation of lightning?

_____

_____

_____

_____

Chemical Change: Polymer Bouncing Ball
Background Information

Classroom Ideas

The Polymer Bouncing Ball is a hands-on activity that can be used to introduce, demonstrate, or reinforce concepts relating to the following topics:

Topics	How the Activity Relates to the Topic
Chemical Change	A chemical change occurs when one or more substances are combined forming a new substance with different properties. A chemical reaction occurs when the glue, borax, and pudding, which have their own properties, are mixed to form a new substance with different properties. The new substance formed is a polymer.
Polymer	The bouncing ball in this activity is made from a polymer. A polymer is a long chain of many molecules strung together. The glue and the pudding mix are polymers. The borax acts as a connecting agent that joins the two polymer chains together. These long polymer chains can be stretched out or balled up, which makes the material elastic.

Related Vocabulary

- **chemical change**: a reaction that transforms a substance into a new substance with different properties
- **chemical property**: a characteristic of a substance that allows it to change to a new substance
- **chemical reaction**: the process in which chemical change occurs
- **compound**: the new substance produced when two or more substances are chemically combined
- **elasticity**: the ability of a stretched substance to return to its original size and shape
- **mixture**: a substance consisting of two or more substances mixed together
- **molecule**: the smallest part of a compound that still has the properties of the compound
- **polymer**: a naturally occurring or synthetic compound consisting of large molecules made up of a linked series of repeated simple monomers
- **solution**: a mixture in which the particles are too small to see

Real-World Connection

The first bouncing balls were made of natural rubber. The "Super Ball" was invented in 1965 by chemist Norman Stingley. The Wham-O company produced them.

Name: _____ Date: _____

Polymer Bouncing Ball

Purpose: Observe a chemical reaction

Materials

vanilla pudding mix

borax

food coloring (optional)

graduated cylinder

2 plastic cups

mL measuring spoons

white glue

water

wooden craft stick

black marking pen

resealable baggie

Procedure

Step #1:   Add 30 mL (2 tablespoons) of water to a plastic cup marked "Solution."

Step #2:   Using a wooden craft stick, stir in 2.5 mL (1/2 teaspoon) of borax.

Step #3:   Mix until borax is dissolved. Set aside.

Step #4:   Thoroughly mix 15 mL (1 tablespoon) of glue with 3 or 4 drops of food coloring in the other plastic cup marked "Mixture."

Step #5:   Stir 10 mL (2 teaspoons) of vanilla pudding mix into the glue mixture.

Step #6:   Now, add 5 mL (1 teaspoon) of the borax solution to the glue mixture.

Step #7:   Blend until mixture sticks to craft stick.

Step #8:   Sprinkle 30 mL (2 tablespoons) of the dry borax onto the countertop.

Step #9:   Pour mixture onto dry borax and knead for 4 minutes.

Step #10: Shape mixture into a ball by rolling in your hands.

Step #11: Bounce your ball!

Step #12: After use, store your ball in a resealable baggie.

Caution: Never eat any of the materials used to make the ball or the ball itself.

Observations

1.   What makes your ball bounce? _____

2.   What sound does your ball make when bounced? _____

3.   How high does your ball bounce? _____

Conclusion

_____

_____

_____

Try

Experiment with different recipes. Mixing in more instant pudding will make a stretchier ball. Use less borax to make a "goopy" kind of ball. Adding more glue will produce a slimier ball.

Acids and Bases: Secret Message
Background Information

Classroom Ideas

Secret Message is a hands-on activity that can be used to introduce, demonstrate, or reinforce concepts relating to the following topics:

Topic	How the Activity Relates to the Topic
Acid and Bases	Goldenrod paper is an acid-base indicator made with dye. Bases are substances with a pH above 7 on the pH scale. The goldenrod paper will turn bright red when the baking soda solution is applied. Acids are substances with a pH below 7 on the pH scale. The goldenrod paper will change back to yellow when the vinegar solution is applied over the base of baking soda solution.

Related Vocabulary

- **acid**: a substance with a pH below 7
- **base (alkaline)**: a substance with a pH above 7
- **indicator**: special paper used to tell if a substance is an acid or a base
- **neutral**: a substance with a pH of 7
- **pH**: a measure of how acidic or basic a solution is; the scale ranges from 0 to 14
- **pH scale**: a tool for measuring acids and bases
- **solution**: a mixture in which the particles are too small to see

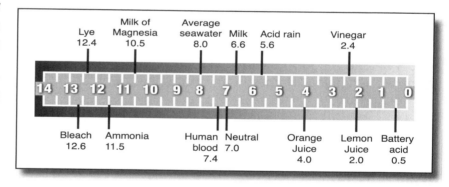

Real-World Connection

The kinds of soils in an area help determine how well crops grow there. Soil can be acid, alkaline, or neutral. Highly acidic or alkaline soils can harm many plants. Changing the pH of a soil is frequently required to grow healthy plants. Most plants grow best within a pH range of 6.5 to 7.2.

Name: _____ Date: _____

Secret Message

Purpose: Observe how acids and bases react to goldenrod paper

Materials

goldenrod indicator paper   cotton swabs
cotton balls   vinegar
baking soda   water
mL measuring spoon
graduated cylinder or measuring cup

Procedure
Part 1
Step #1: Place a sheet of goldenrod indicator paper on a dry surface.
Step #2: Mix 15 mL (1 tablespoon) of baking soda with 125 mL (1/2 cup) of water. Stir until dissolved.
Step #3: Dip a cotton swab into the baking soda mixture and squeeze out excess moisture.
Step #4: Print your name on the goldenrod paper with the swab. Allow time for it to dry.
Step #5: Saturate a cotton ball in the vinegar.
Step #6: Wash it over your name.

Part 2
Step #1: Dip a cotton swab in vinegar.
Step #2: Print your name on another sheet of goldenrod paper with the swab. Allow time for it dry.
Step #3: Saturate a cotton ball in the baking soda mixture.
Step #4: Wash it over your name.

Observations

_____

_____

Conclusion

_____

_____

Try
You can test many household items to determine if they are acidic or alkaline (basic). Try testing milk, soda pop, juice, salad dressing, spaghetti sauce, or any of your favorite foods by applying them to goldenrod indicator paper.

Rocks and Minerals: Briquette Crystals
Background Information

Classroom Ideas

Briquette Crystals is a hands-on activity that can be used to introduce, demonstrate, or reinforce concepts relating to the following topics:

Topics	How the Activity Relates to the Topic
Capillary Action	The porous material (briquettes or sponge pieces) provides a means for capillary action to carry the liquid containing bluing and salt up from the main source of liquid. Once the capillary action brings up the liquid, evaporation occurs that causes additional crystal formations.
Crystallization	Crystallization occurs when salt molecules join together as the liquid evaporates into the air. Crystal formations are speeded up by sprinkling salt on the briquettes.
Evaporation	Evaporation is essential to growing crystals on the briquettes. Although the ammonia helps speed the rate of evaporation, it is also important to avoid direct sunlight because this will cause the liquid to evaporate faster than the growing structure can draw it up. The crystals will form on the plate instead of the porous material. Keep this project in an area with low humidity (warm and dry). This activity works like an evaporating dish recovering dissolved solids.

Related Vocabulary

- **capillary action**: a phenomenon where liquid spontaneously rises in a narrow space such as a thin tube or in porous materials
- **crystal**: a solid composed of atoms arranged in an orderly pattern
- **evaporation**: the slow changing of a liquid into a gas
- **mineral**: a naturally occurring, non-living solid with a specific chemical composition and crystal structure
- **porous**: the capability of physically absorbing liquids
- **rock**: a naturally occurring combination of minerals

Real-World Connection

Bluing has been used since the late 1890s. It is an ionized salt (ferric hexacyanoferrate) bleach alternative also known as Prussian blue that is environmentally safe, biodegradable, and non-toxic. When washing whites, a few drops of bluing are added to the rinse water, turning the water blue. The blue water visually cancels the yellow build-up that occurs in white clothing, making them seem whiter. Today, many laundry detergents and additives are colored blue, but they may not contain bluing.

Name: _____ Date: _____

Briquette Crystals

Purpose: Observe crystals forming

Materials

        charcoal briquettes   liquid bluing
        porous material: cut-up sponge, cork, or brick (optional)
        salt   water   jar
        household ammonia   food coloring
        medium disposable whipped topping or margarine tub
        graduated cylinder   mL measuring spoon

Procedure

Day 1

Step #1: Place briquettes and porous material in disposable margarine tub.

Step #2: In jar, thoroughly mix 2 tablespoons (30 mL) of water, 2 tablespoons (30 mL) of salt, 2 tablespoons (30 mL) of liquid bluing, and 2 tablespoons (30 mL) of household ammonia. *Note*: There will be undissolved salt on the bottom of the solution.

Step #3: Pour solution over porous material.

Step #4: Spoon any remaining salt into the tub as well.

Day 2

Step #5: Sprinkle 2 tablespoons (30 mL) of salt over the porous material.

Day 3

Step #6: Repeat Step #2.

Step #7: Pour mixture into the bottom (not directly on porous material).

Step #8: Add a few drops of food coloring to each piece of porous material. (May use a variety of colors).

Note: To keep the crystals growing, add more of the solution every 2 to 3 days.

Observations

_____

_____

Conclusion

_____

_____

Try

Shape and twist pipe cleaners into flowers and trees. Stick them into the porous sponge to create a stunning crystal garden!

Physical Change: It's in the Bag Ice Cream
Background Information

Classroom Ideas

It's in the Bag Ice Cream is a hands-on activity that can be used to introduce, demonstrate, or reinforce concepts relating to the following topics:

Topics	How the Activity Relates to the Topic
Heat Energy	When the salt is added to the ice, it causes a reaction that moves some energy from the environment to the ice. This causes the ice to melt, and also lowers its freezing point. Water will freeze at 32 degrees Fahrenheit (0 degrees Celsius). Once the salt has been added, the temperature drops below 32 degrees. The liquid ice cream mixture loses heat energy, causing it to get colder and harder.
States of Matter	The ice cream mixture is a liquid before the crushed ice is added. It becomes a solid after the salted ice freezes it.

Related Vocabulary

- **freezing point**: the temperature at which a liquid freezes
- **heat**: the transfer of energy from one object to another
- **liquid**: a substance with a definite volume but no definite shape
- **physical change**: a change in size, shape, or form of matter
- **physical property**: a characteristic of matter that can be observed, such as color, size, shape, taste, texture, and form
- **solid**: a substance that has a definite shape and volume
- **states of matter**: a physical property of matter: solid, liquid, gas, and plasma

Real-World Connection

The first hand-cranked ice cream machine was developed by Nancy Johnson in 1843. The machine worked by filling a can with milk, sugar, and flavoring. It was then placed inside a larger can filled with ice and salt. A crank fitted with a mixing paddle was fitted into the interior can. The ingredients were churned by the paddle as the crank was turned.

Today, ice cream shops can mix much larger batches, and commercial manufacturers make several thousand gallons of ice cream a day in one freezer!

Name: _____ Date: _____

It's in the Bag Ice Cream

Purpose: Observe a liquid change to a solid

Materials

sugar	vanilla extract	milk
half and half	cream	crushed ice
bath towel	rock salt	

graduated cylinder or measuring cup

quart and gallon resealable freezer baggies

Procedure

Step #1: Put 250 mL (1 cup) of milk, 250 mL (1 cup) of half and half, 60 mL (1/4 cup) of sugar, and 5 mL (1 teaspoon) of vanilla in a quart baggie and seal. *Note*: Remove air from the bag before sealing.

Step #2: Place the sealed ingredient baggie inside a gallon baggie.

Step #3: Pack crushed ice in the bigger bag around the quart baggie.

Step #4: Pour 250 mL (1 cup) of rock salt evenly over the ice.

Step #5: Seal the outer baggie. *Note*: Remove air from the bag before sealing.

Step #6: Wrap in the towel to keep hands from freezing.

Step #7: Shake, twist, and massage bags for 8 to 10 minutes.

Step #8: Open the outer baggie and remove the inner baggie.

Step #9: Wipe off the baggie so the salt water doesn't get into the ice cream.

Step #10: Open and spoon the ice cream into cups. Serve plain or top with your favorite toppings.

Note: By double-bagging the inner baggie with another quart baggie, the risk of salt and ice leaking into the ice cream is minimized. Duct tape may also be folded and placed over the seal for extra security. However, the top will have to be cut off after freezing.

Observations

What happened when salt was added to the ice? _____

_____

_____

Conclusion

_____

_____

Try

You can make a bigger batch of ice cream by using a small and large coffee can. Just double the ingredients in the recipe above. Put the mixture in the smaller can and securely seal the lid with duct tape. Then place it in the larger can. Pack the large can with ice and salt, and seal the lid with duct tape. Roll the can back and forth between you and a friend on the ground or sidewalk outside (the condensation will drip) until the ice cream is set. This should take approximately 12 to 15 minutes.

Atoms: Glowing Pickle
Background Information

Classroom Ideas

The Glowing Pickle activity is a teacher demonstration that can be used to reinforce concepts relating to the following topics:

Topics	How the Activity Relates to the Topic
Atoms	Everything in the world is made up of atoms. Atoms connect or bond together into molecules. A molecule can be a new substance, or it can be a common form of an element. For example, sodium atoms and chlorine atoms bond to make sodium chloride (NaCl), known as table salt. Atoms are made up of electrons, protons, and neutrons. When energy is added to electrons in an atom, they give off visible light. Add energy in the form of electricity to the sodium atoms in a pickle, and the pickle will glow or give off light.
Electricity	When an electric current flows through a pickle, it heats the salt-rich water in the pickle above the boiling point near the electrodes (forks). The water is turned to steam and leaves the pickle. A spark leaps between the dry region near one electrode and the electrode still in the wet region. The spark excites the sodium, and yellow light is emitted.

Related Vocabulary

- **atom**: the smallest part of an element
- **chemical bond**: a force that holds two or more atoms together
- **current electricity**: the movement of electrons, which creates the flow of electricity
- **electrical energy**: the energy carried by electric current
- **electricity**: the flow of electrical charges
- **electrode**: a conductor used to make electrical contact with some part of a circuit
- **electron**: a negatively charged particle that travels around the nucleus of an atom
- **element**: a substance made up of only one kind of atom that cannot be divided by ordinary chemical means
- **molecule**: the smallest part of a compound that still has the properties of the compound
- **neutron**: an uncharged particle located in the nucleus of an atom
- **proton**: a positively charged particle in the nucleus of an atom

Real-World Connection

Fireworks get their colors from the salts used to make the explosives. When the atoms of different salts are excited, they emit different colors. The element giving that green color to fireworks is copper (Cu), and the pink color is lithium (Li).

Name: _____ Date: _____

Teacher Demonstration

Caution: Dealing with electricity can be dangerous. Because this activity uses 120 volts of electricity, this activity should be done as a teacher demonstration only.

Purpose: Make a dill pickle glow

Materials

    large dill pickle   2 ring stands
    2 clamps for the ring stands
    2 metal forks   paper towels
    1 six-foot extension cord
    wire strippers   electrical tape
    power strip with an isolated
        switch and fuse

Procedure

Step #1: Set up the ring stands about a foot apart.

Step #2: Connect the forks to the ring stands with the clamps. Make sure the forks' tines are facing each other. (Do not allow the tines of the two forks to touch.)

Step #3: Put the pickle in position. Stick one fork into the pickle past the tines. Then stick the other fork into the pickle.

Step #4: Modify an extension cord. Cut off the outlet section of the cord. Split the cord lengthwise about one meter away from the cut end. Strip both wires about 4 cm from the end, leaving two bare wires.

Step #5: Connect the wires to the forks. Cover with electrical tape.

Step #6: With the power strip unplugged, plug the extension cord into it.

Step #7: Plug the power strip into an electrical outlet. Turn on the power strip.

Step #8: Turn the lights off. After a few seconds, the pickle will start to drip, hiss, and smoke. Then shortly after that, the pickle should start to glow.

Step #9: Unplug the pickle after a few seconds.

Observations

_____

_____

Conclusion

_____

_____

Try

Make brine with Salt Substitute (potassium chloride). Soak a pickle in the brine for a week and then repeat the demonstration. Instead of yellow, the pickle will glow pink from the potassium.

Atmospheric Pressure: Bottled Egg
Background Information

Classroom Ideas

Bottled Egg is a teacher demonstration that can be used to introduce, demonstrate, or reinforce concepts relating to the following topics:

Topic	How the Activity Relates to the Topic
Atmospheric Pressure	The pressure exerted by the atmosphere is called atmospheric pressure. It is caused by the force of gravity. The burning paper heats up the air molecules inside the bottle, causing them to move farther away from each other. Some of the expanding molecules escape past the egg. When the flame dies out, the air molecules inside the bottle move closer together, or contract. The pressure inside the bottle drops, becoming less than the outside air pressure. The air pressure outside the bottle is now greater than the air pressure inside the bottle. The air pressure will try to equalize, forcing the egg into the bottle.

Related Vocabulary

- **atmospheric pressure**: the pressure exerted by the atmosphere
- **force**: a push or a pull
- **gravity**: the force that pulls objects toward each other
- **heat**: the transfer of energy from one object to a cooler object
- **molecule**: the smallest particle of a substance
- **pressure**: a force

Real-World Connection

A barometer is an instrument used by weather forecasters to measure atmospheric pressure. The first barometers were developed in Italy in the 1600s from ideas formulated by Galileo. Weather forecasters use the changes in atmospheric pressure to forecast short-term changes in the weather.

Earth's atmospheric pressure is exerting force on every inch of your body. In fact, the force is 14.7 pounds per square inch (1 kilogram per square centimeter). The air inside your body balances out the outside pressure. That's why you're not squished!

Name: _____ Date: _____

Bottled Egg

Purpose: Demonstrate the effects of air pressure

Materials

    medium hard-boiled egg

    glass bottle (milk bottle or wide mouth juice bottle that an egg will not immediately drop into)

    matches   newspaper

Procedure

Caution: Adult supervision is highly recommended for this activity.

Part 1: Egg into the bottle

Step #1: Peel and dry the hard-boiled egg.

Step #2: Tightly twist a 10 cm by 2 cm piece of newspaper.

Step #3: Use the match to light one end of the newspaper and drop it into the bottle.

Step #4: Place the egg, small end down, on the bottle opening.

Part 2: Removing the egg from the bottle

Step #1: Turn the bottle upside down and shake out loose debris.

Step #2: Adjust the egg with the small end resting in the bottle opening.

Step #3: Tilt the bottle slightly and forcefully blow air in.

Step #4: Hold the bottle upside down and the egg will fall out.

Observations

What happens to the egg before it is sucked into the bottle? _____

_____

_____

Conclusion

Why did the egg get sucked into the bottle?_____

_____

_____

Try

Fill a small balloon with water so that it is slightly wider than the mouth of the bottle and tie a knot in the balloon. Wet the outside of the balloon with a little water. Light a piece of twisted newspaper and drop it into the bottle. Place the balloon on top of the bottle. Watch what happens.

Light: Bubble Observatory
Background Information

Classroom Ideas

The Bubble Observatory is an engineering activity that can be used to introduce, demonstrate, or reinforce concepts relating to the following topics:

Topics	How the Activity Relates to the Topic
White Light	White light contains all the colors of the rainbow. Colors seen in the soap bubble come from white light. Some colors get brighter, and others disappear when light reflects from the soap bubble.
White Light Wave Frequency	The light waves in white light are made of many different frequencies. Frequency of a light wave determines which color light you see. The frequency measures how many electromagnetic vibrations happen in a second. The highest frequency light, violet, vibrates 723,000 times in a billionth of a second.
Interference Colors	Interference colors depend on how far light waves have to travel before they meet up again. This depends on the distance between the layers or thickness of the soap film. Each color corresponds to a certain thickness of the soap film. A soap bubble looks black just before it pops, when the soap film is one-millionth of an inch thick. Interference colors look brightest on the surface of the bubble when there is white light shining on the bubble and a black background behind it. Colors come from the light reflected from the soap bubble.
Surface Tension	Surface tension helps a drop of water hold its shape. Water molecules form bonds that hold them together, forming an invisible "skin" on the surface of the water. When liquid dish soap is added to water, it increases surface tension, allowing you to blow big bubbles.

Related Vocabulary

- **color**: the property of reflecting light of a particular wavelength
- **electromagnetic spectrum**: the range of electromagnetic waves, including radio waves, visible light, and X-rays, with different frequencies and wavelengths
- **electromagnetic wave**: a wave of vibrating electric and magnetic fields
- **frequency**: the number of wavelengths that pass a given point in a certain time
- **interference**: the phenomenon that occurs when two waves meet while traveling along the same medium
- **reflection**: the light energy bouncing off an object or surface
- **surface tension**: a property of liquid surfaces that causes the surface layer to behave like a thin elastic 'skin'

Real-World Connection

Bubbles are a sphere of gas surrounded by a thin film of liquid. Anti-bubbles are a sphere of liquid surrounded by a thin film of gas. Anti-bubbles are formed by slowly dripping water into a full sink. However, they do not last long, so they are hard to see.

Name: _____ Date: _____

Bubble Observatory

Purpose: Construct a Bubble Observatory to observe the colors in bubbles

Materials

working flashlight   plastic tape (clear)
small, clear plastic lid   spoon
darkened room   straw   measuring cup

Materials for Bubble Mix

large dishpan   water   dishwashing liquid

Procedure

Step #1: In a large dishpan, mix 1 gallon of water and 2/3 cup of dishwashing soap. Set aside.

Step #2: Tape the plastic lid over the lens cover of the flashlight with the lip of the lid facing up away from the flashlight.

Step #3: Point the flashlight straight up and turn it on.

Step #4: Wet the lid by dipping your finger in the bubble mix and rubbing it on the lid.

Step #5: Place 1 to 2 spoonfuls of bubble mix on the lid.

Step #6: Use the straw to blow a bubble dome that covers the entire lid.

Step #7: In the darkened room, hold the flashlight so that the bottom of the dome is just above your eyebrows.

Step #8: Watch the colors as they blend and spin around. To move the colors, put your wet straw into the dome and gently blow.

Observations

1. How many colors do you see? _____

2. Do the colors change? _____

3. Just before the bubble pops, what color or colors do you see? _____

Conclusion

_____

_____

_____

Try

Experiment making bubble prints. Mix different colors of tempera paint in with your bubble solution. Then, after blowing bubbles, press paper against the bubbles. The bubbles will pop against the paper. This 'preserves' the bubbles, allowing you plenty of time to study the shapes bubbles form.

Sound: Squawking String
Background Information

Classroom Ideas

Squawking String is an engineering activity that can be used to introduce, demonstrate, or reinforce concepts relating to the following topics:

Topics	How the Activity Relates to the Topic
Sound	Sound is energy transferred by an object vibrating in the air. Friction is created as your finger rubs and slides down the string; this causes the string to vibrate. Sound is produced by these vibrations. The cup works like a speaker, amplifying the sound as the vibrations move up to the cup.
Properties of Sound	The properties of sound—amplitude, loudness, frequency, and pitch—can all be taught with this activity. The rubbing and sticking of your fingers down the string causes amplitude of the sound wave; the greater the amplitude, the louder the sound. When the string is being pulled quickly, the frequency and pitch are higher. *Note*: Loudness and pitch are not connected. High-pitched sounds can be soft; low-pitched sounds can be loud.

Related Vocabulary

- **amplitude**: the maximum height of a wave crest or depth of a trough
- **crest**: the high point of a wave
- **decibel**: a unit that measures the loudness of different sounds
- **frequency**: the number of wavelengths that pass a given point in a certain time
- **friction**: a force that acts to oppose sliding that occurs between two surfaces that are touching
- **loudness**: the human perception of how much energy a sound wave carries
- **pitch**: highness or lowness of sound, determined by the frequency of the wave
- **trough**: the low point on a wave
- **vibration**: the repetition of back and forth or up and down motion
- **wavelength**: the distance between the top of one crest to the top of the next crest (or from trough to trough)

Real-World Connection

Stringed instruments like guitars and violins are played by pressing your fingers down on the strings while you strum, pluck, or bow them. This changes the length of the strings, which causes them to vibrate at different frequencies, causing different sounds. When the string shortens, the sound gets higher.

Name: _____   Date: _____

Squawking String

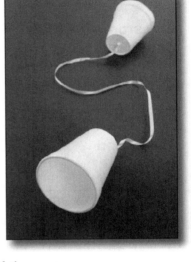

Purpose: Construct an instrument that amplifies sound

Materials

small paperclip   tape
scissors   large plastic cup
sharpened pencil   water
piece of kite string (60 cm long)

Procedure

Step #1:   Use the sharpened pencil tip to poke a small hole in the
             bottom center of the plastic cup.
Step #2:   Thread the string through the hole.
Step #3:   Tie a small paperclip to the end inside the cup.
Step #4:   Pull the string so the paperclip fits snuggly to the bottom of the cup.
Step #5:   Tape the clip flatly on the bottom.
Step #6:   Wet the string with water.
Step #7:   Hold the cup upright in one hand with the string dangling down. With the other hand,
             pinch the string between your finger and thumb near the bottom of the cup.
Step #8:   Quickly slide your fingers down the string.
Step #9:   It may take a few tries, but shortly, your cup will squawk!

Observations

1.   What sound is heard when you pull the string quickly? _____

2.   Pull the string slowly. What do you hear? _____

3.   What sound do you hear if you shorten the length of string? _____

Conclusion

_____

_____

Try

Make a string phone. Connect two large plastic cups with a long piece of string. One person
talks into his or her cup while the other person listens in his or her cup. When you are
communicating with your friend, remember to keep the string tight and in a straight line for a
good connection.

Motion: Balloon-Powered Racer
Background Information

Classroom Ideas

The Balloon-Powered Racer is an engineering activity that can be used to introduce, demonstrate, or reinforce concepts relating to the following topics:

Topics	How the Activity Relates to the Topic
Motion	Motion is the act of moving from one place to another. Newton's Laws of Motion explain the relationship between force and motion. The Balloon Racer can be used to demonstrate Newton's Third Law of Motion. When the balloon is released, the air is forced through the straw at one end of the racer, and that pushes the racer with equal force in the opposite direction.
Friction	Friction occurs anytime two surfaces slip, slide, or move against one another. Surface friction is caused by the irregularities between touching surfaces. Even surfaces that appear to be very smooth are irregular when viewed microscopically. The irregularities obstruct motion. The amount of friction acting between two surfaces depends on the kinds of material from which the two surfaces are made. Surface friction is reduced in this activity by the wheels and the smooth, tiled surface used to test the racer.

Related Vocabulary

- **action**: a force (push or pull) that causes another equal but opposite force
- **friction**: a force that resists motion
- **motion**: the act of moving from one place to another
- **Newton's Third Law of Motion (Law of Action and Reaction)**: states that for every action there is an equal and opposite reaction
- **reaction**: a force (push or pull) in the opposite direction caused by an action force
- **surface friction**: a force that resists motion when two surfaces touch or rub against one another

Real-World Connection

The Balloon-Powered Racer works on the same principle that makes real rocket engines work in space. The engine pushes out hot gasses from the combustion inside, and that pushes the rocket forward in space.

Name: _____   Date: _____

Balloon-Powered Racer

Purpose: Construct a balloon-powered racer

Materials

straight pins   masking tape   flexible straws   balloon
scissors   ink pen   Styrofoam tray
a variety of different-sized round plastic lids

Procedure

Step #1: On the tray, draw a racer body, trace around a plastic lid to draw the 4 tires, and draw 4 smaller circles for the hubs.

Step #2: Cut out the racer parts from the Styrofoam tray. Push the pins through the hubs into the wheels and then into the edges of the racer body.

Step #3: Stretch the balloon by blowing it up and letting the air out. Raise the short end of the flex straw. Place the balloon mouth over the short end of the flexible straw. Tape the balloon securely to the straw.

Step #4: Place the straw lengthwise on the body of the racer. Allow 2 cm of the open end of the straw to reach beyond the back end of the body. Tape the straw to the body of the racer.

Step #5: Blow up the balloon through the straw. Squeeze the end of the straw. Place the racer on a smooth surface, such as a tiled or wooden floor, and let it go. Measure and record the distance traveled in centimeters in the data table below.

Step #6: Test your balloon racer 2 more times and record the results.

Step #7: Calculate the average distance traveled by your racer. Record the distance in the data table.

Results: Measure and record the distance traveled in centimeters in the data table below.

Trial #1	Trial #2	Trial #3	Average Distance Traveled

Conclusion

_____

_____

Try

Design, construct, and test a new balloon racer based on the results of your first racer. Modify your racer by using a different body shape, different-sized balloon, or number, size, and placement of the wheels.

Friction: Air Cushion Vehicle
Background Information

Classroom Ideas

The Air Cushion Vehicle is an engineering activity that can be used to introduce, demonstrate, or reinforce concepts relating to the following topics:

Topics	How the Activity Relates to the Topic
Friction	The hovercraft floats above the floor on a cushion of air provided by the balloon. The air moving through the holes in the plastic sheeting on the air cushion vehicle forms a layer of air between the vehicle and the floor. This reduces friction that would have existed if the hovercraft rested directly on the floor. With less friction, the hovercraft moves across the floor.
Air Pressure	The hovercraft acts on the principles of pressure. The air moving through the holes in the plastic sheeting on the air cushion vehicle forms a layer of air between the vehicle and the floor. The air serves as an invisible cushion that eliminates almost all friction between the vehicle and the surface.

Related Vocabulary

- **action**: a force (push or pull) that causes an equal but opposite force
- **friction**: a force that resists motion
- **hovercraft**: an air cushion vehicle (ACV) that travels on a layer of compressed air just above any kind of surface—land or water
- **motion**: the act of moving from one place to another
- **Newton's Third Law of Motion (Law of Action and Reaction)**: states that for every action there is an equal and opposite reaction
- **pressure**: a force applied to a surface
- **reaction**: a force (push or pull) in the opposite direction caused by an action force
- **surface friction**: a force that resists motion when two surfaces touch or rub against one another

Real-World Connection

A hockey puck moves over the ice using the same principles that move a hovercraft. A very thin layer of air between the puck and the ice results in very little resistance.

Hovercrafts can have many applications. They are unique as transportation vehicles because they are amphibious: they can move over land and water. Hovercrafts or Air Cushion Vehicles (ACV) can carry passengers, vehicles, and freight. Some ACV's can travel as fast as 80 miles per hour.

Name: _____ Date: _____

Air Cushion Vehicle

Purpose: Construct an Air Cushion Vehicle

Materials

1 leaf blower or 1 large Shop Vac with reverse switch
100-ft. extension cord   electric drill
staple gun and staples   plastic lid from a coffee can
jigsaw   one sheet of 3⁄4-inch thick plywood
open, tiled floor   one 1-inch long, 1⁄4-inch bolt and nut
duct tape   1 sheet of heavy plastic, larger than the plywood

Procedure

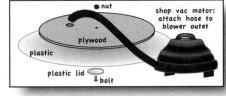

Step #1:   Cut a circle with a 4-foot diameter from the plywood.

Step #2:   Drill a 1⁄4-inch hole in the center of the plywood.

Step #3:   Cut a 2-inch hole (or a size that matches the end of the leaf blower/Shop Vac hose) halfway between the center and the outer edge of the circle.

Step #4:   Cut a circle with a diameter of 6 feet from the plastic sheet (or a circle large enough to cover the bottom of the plywood and fold over the edge of the plywood circle).

Step #5:   Place the plywood on top of the plastic. Fold the edges of the plastic sheet up over the plywood, and then staple it to the top of the plywood disk. Leave some slack in the plastic. When inflated, the plastic will fill with air and lift the rider up off the floor. Seal the stapled plastic by taping around the perimeter with duct tape.

Step #6:   Turn the plywood over. Cut six 1-inch holes in the plastic covering the bottom. The holes should be evenly spaced about halfway between the center and outer edge of the plywood. If they are too far from the center, the floor may block them, preventing air from escaping. (If you make a mistake, cover the hole with duct tape.)

Step #7:   Punch a hole in the plastic coffee can lid and push the bolt through the hole. Push the bolt through the plastic, then through the center hole in the plywood. Fasten with the nut. This will give a billowing doughnut effect to the plastic when inflated. Cover the bolt with duct tape. (When in use, the plastic may rip over the plastic lid. Just repair with duct tape.)

Step #8:   Place the hose of the Shop Vac or leaf blower in the 2-inch hole.

Step #9:   Sit in the center of the plywood. (You may have to shift your weight to make the hovercraft level.) Turn on the air supply. Give the hovercraft a little push and it will float across the floor. Turn the air supply off before the rider gets off the hovercraft.

Conclusion

_____

_____

Try

Experiment with the placement and number of holes in the plastic. Try the hovercraft on a tiled inclined plane.

Electricity: Electronic Quiz Game
Background Information

Classroom Ideas

The Electronic Quiz Game is an engineering activity that can be used to introduce, demonstrate, or reinforce concepts relating to the following topics:

Topics	How the Activity Relates to the Topic
Energy	There are many forms of energy, but they can all be put into two groups: potential and kinetic. The battery is an example of potential, or stored, energy. Electrical energy is stored in a battery and used to power the Electronic Quiz Game.
Electricity	Electrical energy is stored in a battery and used to power the Electronic Quiz Game. Electrical energy is delivered by electrons, or tiny charged particles, moving through a wire from the battery to the light bulb. The light bulb lights up when the circuit is complete.
Current Electricity	The movement of electrons in the wire connected to the battery creates the flow of electricity that provides the energy to operate the game.
Electrical Circuits	The game uses a circuit to convert electrical energy into light energy. The light bulb lights up when you have a complete, or closed, circuit. This is the case when you have selected a matched pair on the quiz board. If you select the wrong match, the path for the electricity is not complete, since the wire and fastener do not connect the bulbs on an incorrect match. When you make the wrong match, the light bulb will not light up.

Related Vocabulary

- **battery**: an energy source
- **current electricity**: the movement of electrons, which creates the flow of electricity
- **conductor**: material capable of transmitting electricity or heat
- **electrical circuit**: a complete path through which electrons flow from an energy source, through a conducting wire and appliance, and back to the energy source
- **electrical energy**: the energy carried by electric current
- **electricity**: the flow of electrical charges
- **insulator**: material capable of preventing the transfer of electricity or heat
- **parallel circuit**: the electrical current can flow through more than one path to make a complete circuit
- **potential energy**: stored energy
- **series circuit**: the electrical current flows through all the devices in the circuit in just one path to make a complete circuit
- **switch**: used to open and close circuits

Real-World Connection

Turning on the lights in a room requires the use of a circuit. Radios, computers, and nearly all electrical devices use circuits.

Name: _____ Date: _____

Electronic Quiz Game

Purpose: Create a game using electricity

Materials

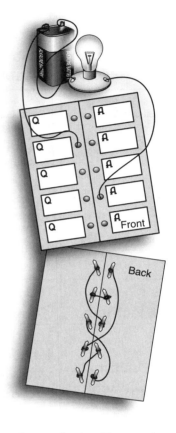

manila file folder   pen
scissors   brass paper fasteners
wire   battery
bulb   bulb holder
glue   paper

Procedure

Step #1: Cut 10 2″ x 3″ cards from paper. Place five cards in one stack and five in another. Take one stack and write one question about electricity on each card. Use the other stack to write an answer on each card for each question.

Step #2: Open the file folder. On the left side of the folder glue the question cards. On the right side, glue the answer cards. Mix them up so each question is across from the wrong answer.

Step #3: Push a paper fastener through the folder next to each question and each answer.

Step #4: Turn the quiz board over and connect each question to the right answer with a piece of wire. Loop the wire around the back of the paper fasteners.

Step #5: With some more wire, connect the battery to the bulb holder as shown in the illustration above.

Step #6: Attach more wire to the other side of the battery and the other side of the bulb holder. Leave the ends of both of these wires free.

Play the Game

Trade games with a partner. Ask your partner to hold one of the loose wires on a paper fastener next to a question and the other loose wire on a paper faster next to the answer they think is the correct one. If they are right, they will complete a circuit and the bulb will light up.

Observations

_____

_____

Conclusion

_____

_____

Bernoulli's Principle: Squeeze Bottle Rocket Launcher
Background Information

Classroom Ideas

The Squeeze Bottle Rocket Launcher is an engineering activity that can be used to introduce, demonstrate, or reinforce concepts relating to the following topics:

Topics	How the Activity Relates to the Topic
Bernoulli's Principle	Bernoulli's Principle explains that an aircraft achieves lift because of the shape of its wings. The wings are shaped so that air flows faster over the top of the wing and slower underneath. Fast-moving air equals low air pressure, while slow-moving air equals high air pressure. The high air pressure underneath the wings pushes the aircraft up through the lower air pressure.
Atmospheric Pressure	The air around us is constantly pushing in on us. This is called atmospheric pressure. We don't notice this pressure because it pushes in equally from all directions. When you squeeze the bottle launcher, the air inside is compressed. This increases the air pressure in the bottle and inside the rocket. The difference in pressure between the inside and the outside creates a force, which pushes the rocket off the end of the launcher. Once the rocket is launched, the air keeps coming out of the opening until the air pressure inside and outside the bottle is the same.
Newton's Third Law of Motion	According to Newton's Third Law, for every action there is an equal and opposite reaction. As you squeeze the bottle, air is forced out of the straw and pushes against the clay plug in the larger straw. The resulting force causes the straw to launch through the air.

Related Vocabulary

- **action**: a force (push or pull) that causes another equal but opposite force
- **atmospheric pressure**: the pressure exerted by the atmosphere
- **Bernoulli's Principle**: in fluid flow, an increase in velocity causes a decrease in pressure, this means the faster a fluid flows, the less pressure it exerts
- **compress**: apply pressure
- **force**: a push or a pull
- **Newton's Third Law of Motion (Law of Action and Reaction)**: for every action there is an equal and opposite reaction
- **pressure**: a force
- **reaction**: a force (push or pull) in the opposite direction caused by an action force

Real-World Connection

A real rocket works using Newton's Third Law of Motion, which says that if something pushes on something else, the other object pushes back just as hard. In a rocket, fuel is burned in a combustion chamber, which is open at one end. As the fuel burns, it produces hot gases that rush out the open end of the chamber. Since the gases are being pushed in one direction by the rocket, the rocket is pushed in the opposite direction with equal force.

Name: _____ Date: _____

Squeeze Bottle Rocket Launcher

Purpose: Construct a squeeze bottle rocket launcher

Materials

      plastic drink bottle with a small opening
      several straws with different diameters
      modeling clay   paper
      tape   scissors

Procedure

Step #1: Construct the launcher first. Place a thin straw partway into the bottle and seal around it with the modeling clay.

Step #2: Construct the rocket. Cut one of the straws with a larger diameter in half. Seal one end by pushing a lump of modeling clay into it.

Step #3: Launch your rocket. Slide the rocket over the straw sticking out of the launcher. Aim the rocket up. Squeeze the bottle hard. **Caution**: Do not aim it at another person or animal.

Step #4: Add paper wings and a nose cone to the straw rocket and launch again.

Observations

_____

_____

Conclusion

_____

_____

Try

Attach different shapes to the straw to see how it affects the flight of the rocket.

Fins	
Tail	

Machines: Mousetrap Racer
Background Information

Classroom Ideas

The Mousetrap Racer is an engineering activity that can be used to introduce, demonstrate, or reinforce concepts relating to the following topics:

Topics	How the Activity Relates to the Topic
Machines	A machine is any device that makes doing work easier. They reduce the force you have to apply to do the work. There are two types of machines: simple and compound. The Mousetrap Racer is a compound machine made up of several simple machines: wheel and axle, lever, and pulley.
Motion	Motion is the act of moving from one place to another. Newton's Laws of Motion explain the relationship between force and motion. The Mousetrap Racer demonstrates Newton's First Law (Law of Inertia). The racer is at rest. When the lever is released, it applies a pulling force on the string. This causes the axle to turn. By turning the axle, the wheels, which are attached to the axle, rotate. Inertia is overcome, and the racer will move forward.
Energy	Mechanical energy is the energy an object has because of its motion or position. The racer is a purely mechanical device that moves without the use of combustible fuel or electricity. The Mousetrap Racer uses two kinds of mechanical energy: kinetic and potential. When the stored energy in the spring of the mousetrap is released, it moves the lever arm, transforming the potential energy into kinetic energy that moves the racer forward.

Related Vocabulary

- **action**: a force (push or pull) that causes another equal but opposite force
- **compound machine or complex machine**: a machine that has two or more simple machines working together to make work easier
- **force**: a push or pull on an object
- **friction**: a force that resists movement between two surfaces
- **inertia**: the tendency of an object at rest to stay at rest or a moving object to keep moving
- **kinetic energy**: the energy an object has because it is moving
- **motion**: the act of moving from one place to another
- **Newton's First Law of Motion (Law of Inertia)**: states an object at rest stays at rest until acted upon by another force; it stays in motion in a straight line at a constant speed until acted upon by another force
- **potential energy**: the energy an object has when it is at rest (stored energy) and depends on the object's position or shape
- **reaction**: a force (push or pull) in the opposite direction caused by an action force

Real-World Connection

Almost every machine built since the beginning of the Industrial Revolution uses the wheel.

Name: _____ Date: _____

Mousetrap Racer

Purpose: Construct a mousetrap racer

Materials

mousetrap	exacto knife
30 cm thread	glue
4 wheels (same size)	2 plastic straws
2 dowels with a smaller diameter than the straws	
1 piece of balsa wood wider and longer than the mousetrap	

Caution: adult supervision required for using an exacto knife.

Procedure

Step #1:   Construct the balsa chassis. Place the mousetrap onto the piece of balsa wood about one inch from one end. This end will be the rear of the vehicle.

Step #2:   Position the mousetrap so that the lever will pull back to the rear. Glue the trap to the balsa wood.

Step #3:   Make a small rectangle opening in the rear of the balsa wood just above where the axle will be placed.

Step #4:   Assemble the wheels and the axle. Cut the dowels and straws to fit the width of the chassis.

Step #5:   Insert the dowel into the straw. Spin the dowel to ensure it will turn easily. Glue the wheels to the dowels. Glue one set of axles to the front of the Mousetrap racer.

Step #6:   Before attaching the rear axle, cut away the middle part of the straw. Glue the rear axle in place. Next, tie the thread to the dowel and wrap the thread around the dowel. Leave one end free to tie to the mousetrap lever.

Step #7:   Tie the lose end of the thread to the mousetrap lever. Pull back the mousetrap lever and lock it into place. Spring the trap and watch your racer go.

Conclusion

_____

_____

Try

Using this basic design, make changes that will improve the performance of your racer. Try different size wheels, different chassis shapes, or increase the distance between the mousetrap and the rear axle.

Gravity: Egg Drop Contraption
Background Information

Classroom Ideas

The Egg Drop Contraption is an engineering activity that can be used to introduce, demonstrate, or reinforce concepts relating to the following topics:

Topics	How the Activity Relates to the Topic
Gravity	Sir Isaac Newton developed the law of gravitation. According to Newton's Law, every object in the universe attracts every other object. He called the force of attraction between the egg contraption and Earth *gravitational attraction*. The amount of gravitational attraction between objects depends on how much mass the objects have and how far apart the objects are.
Motion	Motion is the act of moving from one place to another. Isaac Newton is the English scientist who stated the three Laws of Motion in 1687. The Laws were named after him. • First Law of Motion: since the egg was in motion, it would have continued in motion if it weren't for the action of an outside force. The floor provides that force. • Second Law of Motion: the floor is the outside force that causes a deceleration. Since the egg comes to a stop quickly, the deceleration has a large magnitude (the outside force is larger than the egg's weight). • Third Law of Motion: since the floor exerts a large force on the egg at impact, the egg exerts an equal and opposite force on the floor. The keys to the egg's survival are to make a contraption that makes the egg's stop less sudden and distributes the force on the egg evenly over its surface.

Related Vocabulary

- **deceleration**: a decrease or negative change in speed or velocity
- **gravity**: a force of attraction that causes objects to fall toward the center of the earth
- **motion**: the act of moving from one place to another
- **Newton's First Law of Motion (Law of Inertia)**: states an object at rest stays at rest until acted upon by another force; an object in motion stays in motion in a straight line at a constant speed until acted upon by another force
- **Newton's Second Law of Motion (Law of Acceleration)**: acceleration depends on the mass of an object and the force pushing or pulling the object
- **Newton's Third Law of Motion (Law of Action and Reaction)**: for every action there is an equal and opposite reaction

Real-World Connection

Proper packaging ensures that products arrive at the store in good working order. Some kinds of packaging used today include foam peanuts, clamshell plastic encasing, and bubble wrap.

Name: _____ Date: _____

Egg Drop Contraption

Purpose: Construct a structure that will keep a raw egg from cracking when dropped from 10 feet

Materials

16 flex straws
1 raw egg
1 meter of masking tape
2 pieces of construction paper
plastic sheeting

3 paper clips
1 meter of string
3 rubber bands
10 craft sticks
paper towels

Procedure

Step #1: Assemble a team of 4 or 5 members.

Step #2: In thirty minutes, construct a structure with an egg inside, using only the materials listed. (Think about creating a design that would reduce the amount of deceleration and cushion the egg upon impact.)

Step #3: When time expires, meet the other teams at the drop site.

Step #4: Cover the drop site with plastic.

Step #5: One member from each team will drop the egg structure from a height of 10 feet. After the egg is dropped, one team member will inspect the structure to see if the egg survived. (You must be able to remove the egg after the structure is dropped without damage.)

Step #6: One member of each team will clean up and remove all items from the drop site before another team drops.

Observations

_____

_____

Conclusion

_____

_____

Try

If your egg did not survive the drop, continue experimenting with your design until you create a structure that protects the egg from breaking during the drop. This may take many different tries to get right—so don't worry if the eggs break over and over again!

Density: Pop Bottle Lava Lamp
Background Information

Classroom Ideas

The Pop Bottle Lava Lamp is an engineering activity that can be used to introduce, demonstrate, or reinforce concepts relating to the following topics:

Topics	How the Activity Relates to the Topic
Density	The Pop Bottle Lava Lamp demonstrates that water is denser (heavier) than oil, which is why the water sinks to the bottom when you pour it in. This is why oil floats on top of the water if a ship spills oil in the ocean.
Molecules	Briskly shaking the Pop Bottle Lava Lamp causes the oil to break up into smaller droplets but not to mix with the water. This is because of molecular polarity. Simply put, molecules of water are attracted to other water molecules, and oil molecules are attracted to other oil molecules. The structure of the two different molecules does not allow them to bond together. The food coloring mixes with the water but does not mix with the oil.
Gases	When the Alka-Seltzer™ tablet connects with the water, it reacts, creating tiny bubbles of carbon dioxide gas. As the gas rises, it attaches to some of the colored water. After the gas bubbles reach the top, they pop. The carbon dioxide has escaped and the food coloring sinks back to the bottom. The Pop Bottle Lava Lamp works because tiny droplets of liquid join together to make one big blob that looks like lava.

Related Vocabulary

- **density**: a measure of the amount of matter contained by a given volume
- **fluid**: any material, either liquid or gas, that can flow
- **gas**: matter with no definite shape or volume
- **intermolecular polarity**: the force between two molecules
- **molecule**: the simplest structural unit of an element or compound

Real-World Connection

In 2010, the catastrophic explosion on British Petroleum's Deepwater Horizon oil rig in the Gulf of Mexico spilled thousands of gallons of oil in the Gulf of Mexico. It was estimated that over 50,000 barrels per day were escaping from the well just before it was capped. For months, miles of oil floated on top of the Gulf waters. The oil slick became the nation's worst environmental disaster in decades. It threatened hundreds of species of fish, birds, and other wildlife along the Gulf Coast.

Name: _____ Date: _____

Pop Bottle Lava Lamp

Purpose: Construct a lava lamp

Materials

clean, clear plastic 20-oz. pop bottle with cap
food coloring   vegetable oil
water   Alka-Seltzer™ tablet
glitter (optional)

Procedure

Step #1: Fill the bottle half full with water.
Step #2: Add 8 to 10 drops of food coloring.
Step #3: Add the vegetable oil, leaving an inch of space at the top of the bottle.
Step #4: Break the Alka-Seltzer™ tablet into 6 to 8 pieces.
Step #5: Drop a piece of the broken tablet into the oil and water mixture.
Step #6: When the bubbling action stops, add another piece of the Alka-Seltzer™ tablet.
Step #7: After the bubbling action stops, screw the cap on.
Step #8: Rock the bottle back and forth. Watch as the liquid droplets join making one big blob.

Note: The lamp will work as long as it takes the Alka-Seltzer™ tablet to dissolve in the water, but you can add more.

Observations

_____

_____

Conclusion

_____

_____

Try

For a cooler visual effect, use a flashlight in a dark room to illuminate your lamp. Simply place the beam under the bottle after you drop in a piece of the tablet.

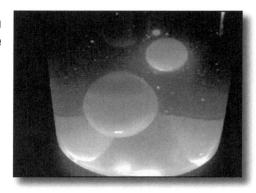

Sorbents: Oil Spill Clean-Up
Background Information

Classroom Ideas

Oil Spill Clean-Up is an experiment that can be used to introduce, demonstrate, or reinforce concepts relating to the following topics:

Topics	How the Activity Relates to the Topic
Sorbents	Scientists have come up with creative ways to clean up oil spills. They use sorbents to try to clean up oil spills before they kill wildlife and contaminate habitats. Sorbents are materials that are good at absorbing liquids.
Scientific Method	Scientific inquiry is a process scientists use to find answers to questions they have about the world around them. They use the steps in the scientific method to design and conduct scientific investigations to explore possible answers. The steps in the scientific method are followed in this experiment.
Archimedes' Principle	A body immersed in a fluid experiences a buoyant force equal to the weight of the fluid it displaces. Density is the relationship between the mass and volume of an object. The more closely packed the molecules, the greater the density of the object. Oil floats on top of water. Oil floats on the surface because it is lighter than water. Scientists say that water is denser than oil.
Buoyancy	Oil floats in water, as opposed to sinks, as a result of a force called buoyant force. Buoyancy is the tendency of certain objects to float or rise in fluid. Buoyant force is the upward force exerted on an object that is immersed in a fluid. Buoyant force is caused by the difference in pressure within the fluid. If the buoyant force of oil is equal to the weight of water, the oil will float. Oil is less dense than water, so 1 cubic cm of oil weighs less than 1 cubic cm of water. Therefore, the upward buoyant force on the oil, which is equal to the weight of water displaced, is greater than the downward force of gravity on the oil, also known as the weight of the oil. This inequality of forces causes the oil to rise in the water.
Fluid	A fluid is any material, either liquid or gas, that can flow. All fluids exert pressure as their molecules move around and bump into the surface of other matter. Oil is a fluid. It is a liquid that will float on the surface of water.

Related Vocabulary

- **absorb**: take in
- **Archimedes' Principle**: a body immersed in a fluid experiences a buoyant force equal to the weight of the fluid it displaces
- **buoyancy**: the tendency of certain objects to float or rise in fluid
- **buoyant force**: the upward pressure exerted on an object by a fluid in which the object rests

Related Vocabulary (cont.)

- **density**: the relationship between the mass and volume of an object
- **fluid**: a substance, either liquid or gas, that can flow
- **molecule**: the simplest structural unit of an element or compound
- **scientific method**: the steps used to design and conduct scientific investigations
- **sorbents**: materials that are good at absorbing liquids

Real-World Connection

A coastal area that is contaminated from an oil spill is never completely cleaned; the ecosystem takes many years to rehabilitate and may never return to its pre-spill state.

In 2010, one of the most devastating man-made environmental disasters to ever occur in the United States took place off the shores of the Gulf of Mexico. An offshore drilling rig owned by British Petroleum Company exploded. Millions of gallons of crude oil poured into the ocean. Large quantities of oil washed onto the beaches and wetlands along the Gulf Coast. Skimmer boats, booms, chemicals, and sorbents were all used to contain and clean up the massive spill.

Name: _____ Date: _____

Oil Spill Clean-Up

Purpose: The purpose is a question that asks what you want to learn from the investigation. 1) It should be clearly written, (2) it usually starts with the verb "Does," and (3) it can be answered by measuring something.

Purpose: Does the type of material used affect the amount of oil removed from water?

Research: The goal of the research is to find information that will help you make a prediction about what will occur in your experiment. Investigate density, buoyancy, oil spills, and sorbents. Use the lines below for note taking.

_____

_____

_____

_____

_____

_____

_____

_____

_____

_____

Hypothesis: Make an educated guess about what you think will happen in your project. Your hypothesis should be clearly written. It should answer the question stated in the purpose, be brief and to the point, and identify the independent and dependent variables.

> *Example*: The type of material (choose one) will / will not affect the amount
> of oil removed from water.

Hypothesis: _____

_____

_____

_____

_____

Name: _____ Date: _____

Procedure: The procedure is a plan for your experiment. The plan includes a list of the materials needed, step-by-step directions (written like a recipe) for conducting the experiment, and identifies the variables. Measurements are made and recorded using metric units.

Materials Needed:

newspaper	large plastic garbage bag	two 1,000-mL graduated cylinders
paper towel	straw or hay	cotton balls
scissors	12 bowls or containers	1 gallon vegetable oil
water	dry measuring cup	liquid soap
stopwatch	mesh coffee filter (found in stores that sell coffee supplies)	

Variables: Variables are often referred to as factors, traits, or conditions. The independent variable is the factor that is changed in an experiment. The dependent variable is the factor that responds to the change. The change is measured and recorded in metric units. Write the independent and dependent variables in this experiment below.

Independent: _____

Dependent: _____

Experiment: The experiment is a test designed to answer the question stated in the purpose. The test consists of two groups.

Controlled Setup: The standard or part of the experiment used for comparison.

Step #1: Spread newspapers onto work surface.

Step #2: Pour 750 mL of water into the graduated cylinder.

Step #3: Slowly add 250 mL of oil. (If a bubble layer forms between the water and oil, pour out the mixture or wait until the bubbles disappear.)

Step #4: The measurements of the oil and water levels have been recorded in the data table for you.

Experimental Setup: The parts of the experiment that are changed and tested.

Step #1: Pour 750 mL of water into the graduated cylinder.

Step #2: Slowly add 250 mL of oil. (If a bubble layer forms between the water and oil, pour out the mixture or wait until the bubbles disappear.)

Step #3: Cut cotton balls into 1- to 2-cm pieces. Place three bowls on the work surface. Place 1 cup of cut cotton balls (sorbent) in each bowl.

Step #4: Place 1 cup of the sorbent in the filter. Lower it slowly into the water-oil mixture and gently move it from side to side for a few seconds until the sorbent is completely submerged.

Name: _____ Date: _____

Step #5: Start the stop watch. After 30 seconds, lift the filter with the contents of the sorbent inside and hold it just above the surface of the water/oil for 30 seconds to drain.

Step #6: Dump the contents of the mesh strainer into the garbage.

Step #7: Read and record the total water and oil levels.

Step #8: Wash out the filter with soap and water.

Step #9: Add water and oil to the graduated cylinder until you have 750 mL of water and 250 mL of oil. (You do not need to start with fresh oil or water.)

Step #10: Repeat steps 4 through 10 two more times.

Step #11: Add water and oil to the graduated cylinder until you have 750 mL of water and 250 mL of oil. Prepare the straw and paper towel as directed in step 3. Repeat steps 4 through 11 for the straw and paper towel sorbents.

Results: Record measurements and averages in data table in mL.

Control Setup			
Sorbent	**Water Level After Removing Sorbent**	**Oil Level After Removing Sorbent**	**Ratio = Remaining Water / Remaining Oil**
No Sorbent	750 mL	250 mL	750 / 250 or 3 / 1
Experimental Setup			
Sorbent	**Water Level After Removing Sorbent**	**Oil Level After Removing Sorbent**	**Ratio = Remaining Water / Remaining Oil**
Cotton Balls			
Trial #1			
Trial #2			
Trial #3			
Average			
Straw			
Trial #1			
Trial #2			
Trial #3			
Average			
Paper Towel			
Trial #1			
Trial #2			
Trial #3			
Average			

Name: _____ Date: _____

Analysis: Study the results of your experiment. Create a bar graph that will compare the percentages of oil collected in the controlled setup and the experimental setup. Place the water-to-oil ratio on the *y*-axis and the names of the sorbents on the *x*-axis.

Water-to-Oil Ratio of Sorbents

Average Ratio of Water to Oil (mL)
(y-axis)

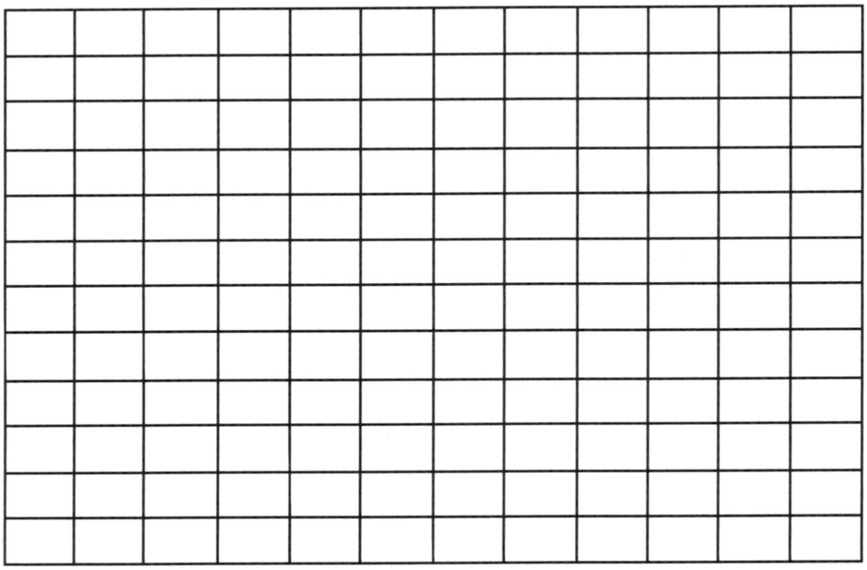

(x-axis)
Sorbents

Conclusion: Write a summary of the experiment (what actually happened). It should include the purpose, a brief description of the procedure, and whether or not the hypothesis was supported by the data collected. Use key facts from your research to help explain the results. The conclusion should be written in first person ("I").

_____

_____

_____

_____

_____

_____

_____

_____

_____

Law of Conservation of Matter: Gas in a Bag
Background Information

Classroom Ideas

Gas in a Bag is an experiment that can be used to introduce, demonstrate, or reinforce concepts relating to the following topics:

Topics	How the Activity Relates to the Topic
Law of Conservation of Matter	The Law of Conservation of Matter is also known as the Law of Conservation of Mass. It states that matter cannot be created or destroyed; it can only change form. This means that the total mass of reactants in a chemical reaction will equal the total mass of products. If a gas is produced during a reaction, its mass is often forgotten when calculating the final mass of the product because students are unable to see the gas. For this experiment, the resealable bag is used to collect the gas and preserve the mass.
Chemical Reaction	A chemical change occurs when one or more substances combine to form a new substance with different properties. A chemical reaction occurs when the vinegar, an acid, reacts with baking soda, a base, to produce a new substance, a salt.
Scientific Method	Scientific inquiry is a process scientists use to find answers to questions they have about the world around them. They use the steps in the scientific method to design and conduct scientific investigations to explore possible answers. The steps in the scientific method are followed in this experiment.

Related Vocabulary

- **chemical change**: a reaction that transforms a substance into a new substance with different properties
- **chemical reaction**: the process by which substances form bonds (or break bonds) and, in doing so, either release or consume energy
- **Law of Conservation of Matter**: matter cannot be created or destroyed; it can only change form
- **mass**: the amount of matter in objects and substances
- **matter**: the term used to describe anything that has mass and takes up space
- **products**: the substances formed during a chemical reaction
- **reactants**: the substances reacting in a chemical reaction
- **scientific method**: the steps used to design and conduct scientific investigations

Real-World Connection

A chemical reaction is the process by which substances form or break bonds, and, in doing so, either release or consume energy. During an ordinary chemical change, there is no detectable increase or decrease in the quantity of matter. Burning a candle is an example of a chemical reaction. The mass of the wick and wax that burned, as well as the oxygen that fed the flame before the reaction, equals the mass of the smoke and the gases released after the reaction.

Name: _____ Date: _____

Gas in a Bag

Purpose: The purpose is a question that asks what you want to learn from the investigation. 1) It should be clearly written, (2) it usually starts with the verb "Does," and (3) it can be answered by measuring something.

Purpose: Does the total mass of reactants in a chemical reaction affect the total mass of the product?

Research: The goal of the research is to find information that will help you make a prediction about what will occur in your experiment. Investigate the law of conservation of matter, chemical reactions, reactants, and products. Use the lines below for note taking.

_____

_____

_____

_____

_____

_____

_____

_____

_____

_____

Hypothesis: Make an educated guess about what you think will happen in your project. Your hypothesis should be clearly written. It should answer the question stated in the purpose, be brief and to the point, and identify the independent and dependent variables.

> *Example*: The total mass of the product will be (chose one) greater than /
> less than / equal to   the total mass of the product.

Hypothesis: _____

_____

_____

_____

_____

Procedure: The procedure is a plan for your experiment. The plan includes a list of the materials needed, step-by-step directions (written like a recipe) for conducting the experiment, and identifies the variables. Measurements are made and recorded using metric units.

Materials Needed:

vinegar   baking soda   large resealable baggies
two plastic cups   balance scale   mL measuring spoons

Variables: Variables are often referred to as factors, traits, or conditions. The independent variable is the factor that is changed in an experiment. The dependent variable is the factor that responds to the change. The change is measured and recorded in metric units. Write the independent and dependent variables in this experiment below.

Independent: _____

Dependent: _____

Experiment: The experiment is a test designed to answer the question stated in the purpose. The test consists of two groups.

<u>Controlled Setup</u>: The standard or part of the experiment used for comparison.
Step #1: Place 250 mL of vinegar in one plastic cup.
Step #2: Place 250 mL of baking soda in the other cup.
Step #3: Place both cups in one resealable plastic baggie. (Do not spill the contents of either cup.)
Step #4: Determine the mass of the cups, contents, and plastic bag. Record the values in the data table below.
Step #5: Carefully pour the vinegar into the baking soda cup. Wait for the reaction to end.
Step #6: Determine the mass of the cups, contents, and plastic bag. Record the values in the data table below.

<u>Experimental Setup</u>: The parts of the experiment that are changed and tested.
Step #7: Repeat steps 1 through 6. Change the amounts of the reactants, vinegar and baking soda, to 150 mL.
Step #8: Repeat steps 1 through 6. Change the amounts of the reactants, vinegar and baking soda, to 75 mL.

Results: Record test results in the data table below and calculate the change in mass.

Test	Beginning Mass (g)	Ending Mass (g)	Change in Mass (g)
Test #1 (Control)			
Test #2			
Test #3			

Name: _____ Date: _____

Analysis: Study the results of your experiment. Create a bar graph that will compare the mass of the reactants to the mass of the product. Place mass in grams on the *y*-axis. Place Tests 1–3 on the *x*-axis.

Compare Mass of Reactants and Products

Mass (g)
(*y*-axis)

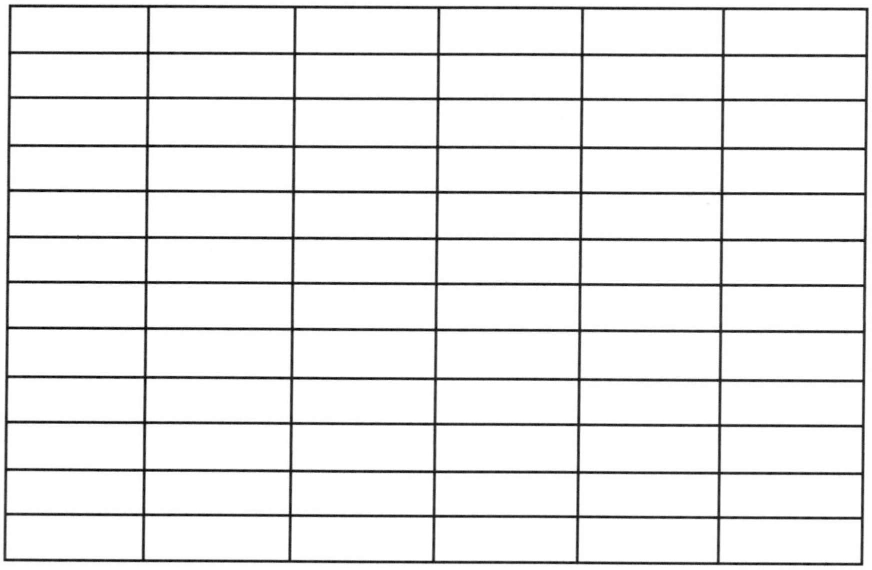

Reactant	Product	Reactant	Product	Reactant	Product
Test #1		Test #2		Test #3	

(*x*-axis)
Total Mass of Reactants and Products

Conclusion: Write a summary of the experiment (what actually happened). It should include the purpose, a brief description of the procedure, and whether or not the hypothesis was supported by the data collected. Use key facts from your research to help explain the results. The conclusion should be written in first person ("I").

_____

_____

_____

_____

_____

_____

_____

_____

Electromagnetic Spectrum: Sunscreen
Background Information

Classroom Ideas
Sunscreen is an experiment that can be used to introduce, demonstrate, or reinforce concepts relating to the following topics:

Topics	How the Activity Relates to the Topic
Electromagnetic Spectrum	Light travels in the form of electromagnetic waves. There are many different types of electromagnetic waves, most of which cannot be detected by the human eye. The full range of electromagnetic waves is called the electromagnetic spectrum. The only part of the electromagnetic spectrum that you can see with your eyes is visible light. Ultraviolet (UV) light is one of the invisible frequencies of light that is given off by the sun. The sun emits ultraviolet radiation, which travels in the form of electromagnetic waves. Overexposure to it can be harmful. Its effects can be seen as sunburn on the skin. Sunscreen helps prevent sunburn caused by UV radiation.
Scientific Method	Scientific inquiry is a process scientists use to find answers to questions they have about the world around them. They use the steps in the scientific method to design and conduct scientific investigations to explore possible answers. The steps in the scientific method are followed in this experiment.

Related Vocabulary

- **electromagnetic spectrum**: the range of electromagnetic waves, including radio waves, visible light, and X-rays, with different frequencies and wavelengths
- **electromagnetic wave**: a wave of vibrating electric and magnetic fields
- **scientific method**: the steps used to design and conduct scientific investigations
- **ultraviolet (UV) light**: one of the invisible frequencies of light that is given off by the sun

Real-World Connection

Overexposure to ultraviolet radiation emitted by the sun can be harmful. Sunscreen helps prevent sunburn caused by UV radiation. All sunscreen lotions have an SPF (Sun Protection Factor) value that correlates with its UV protection.

Name: _____ Date: _____

Sunscreen

Purpose: The purpose is a question that asks what you want to learn from the investigation. 1) It should be clearly written, (2) it usually starts with the verb "Does," and (3) it can be answered by measuring something.

Purpose: Does the SPF level of sunscreen affect the amount of UV radiation absorbed by a UV detecting bead?

Research: The goal of the research is to find information that will help you make a prediction about what will occur in your experiment. Investigate electromagnetic spectrum, ultraviolet radiation, sunscreen SPF, and UV beads. Use the lines below for note taking.

_____

_____

_____

_____

_____

_____

_____

_____

_____

Hypothesis: Make an educated guess about what you think will happen in your project. Your hypothesis should be clearly written. It should answer the question stated in the purpose, be brief and to the point, and identify the independent and dependent variables.

> *Example*: A sunscreen with a higher SPF will (choose one) increase /
> decrease the amount of UV rays absorbed by a substance.

Hypothesis: _____

_____

_____

_____

Name: _____ Date: _____

Procedure: The procedure is a plan for your experiment. The plan includes a list of the materials needed, step-by-step directions (written like a recipe) for conducting the experiment, and identifies the variables. Measurements are made and recorded using metric units.

Materials Needed:
- 1 package of UV detecting beads
- 3 sunscreen lotions (same brand) with different SPF values
- 4 (medium size) resealable baggies

Variables: Variables are often referred to as factors, traits, or conditions. The independent variable is the factor that is changed in an experiment. The dependent variable is the factor that responds to the change. The change is measured and recorded in metric units. Write the independent and dependent variables in this experiment below.

Independent: _____

Dependent: _____

Experiment: The experiment is a test designed to answer the question stated in the purpose. The test consists of two groups.

Controlled Setup: The standard or part of the experiment used for comparison.
Step #1: Divide the package of UV beads equally into the 4 resealable baggies.
Step #2: Label one bag "No sunscreen." This bag will not be coated with sunscreen and will automatically be rated a "5" in the data chart for showing the most dramatic color change.

Experimental Setup: The parts of the experiment that are changed and tested.
Step #1: Coat one baggie with 10 mL of sunscreen and label with the SPF value.
Step #2: Repeat step 1 for the other two baggies and the other two sunscreens.
Step #3: Place the baggies from the Control Setup and Experimental Setup outdoors in direct sunlight.
Step #4: Allow the beads to absorb UV rays for 5 minutes.
Step #5: Rate the bead color on a scale of 1–5, with 5 showing the most dramatic color change or "burning" and 1 showing the least color.

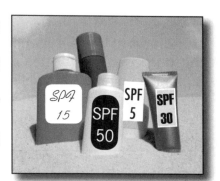

Results: Rate the bead color on a scale of 1–5, with 5 showing the most color or "burning" and 1 showing the least color. Record the ratings in the data table below.

	Control Group	Experimental Group		
Color Rating	**None**	**SPF of ___**	**SPF of ___**	**SPF of ___**
Rating (1–5)	5			

Name: _____ Date: _____

Analysis: Study the results of your experiment. Create a bar graph that will compare the bag of UV beads without sunscreen in the control group with the bags of UV beads with sunscreen in the experimental group. Place the dependent variable (rating of UV bead color) on the *y*-axis. Place the independent variable (SPF value) on the *x*-axis.

Ultraviolet Rays and Sunscreen

Color Rating (1 to 5) (*y*-axis)

(*x*-axis)
SPF Value

Conclusion: Write a summary of the experiment (what actually happened). It should include the purpose, a brief description of the procedure, and whether or not the hypothesis was supported by the data collected. Use key facts from your research to help explain the results. The conclusion should be written in first person ("I").

_____

_____

_____

_____

_____

_____

_____

Evaporation: Instant Snow
Background Information

Classroom Ideas

Instant Snow is an experiment that can be used to introduce, demonstrate, or reinforce concepts relating to the following topics:

Topics	How the Activity Relates to the Topic
Evaporation	Evaporation is the process by which liquid water enters the atmosphere as water vapor. Hydrating the Instant Snow polymer causes it to expand in volume. When Instant Snow is left to dry for several days, the water will evaporate, and it will return to its normal volume.
Osmosis	Instant Snow is made of tiny super-absorbent polymers, which are long chains of molecules linked together. Instant Snow absorbs water and can expand many times its normal size through a process called osmosis, where water molecules pass through a barrier from one side to the other. When water comes in contact with the polymer, it moves from outside the polymer to the inside and causes it to swell. The polymer chains have an elastic quality, but they can stretch only so far and hold only so much water.
Law of Conservation of Matter	The Law of Conservation of Matter is also known as the Law of Conservation of Mass. It states that matter cannot be created or destroyed; it can only change form. Hydrating the Instant Snow polymer causes it to expand in volume. When Instant Snow is left to dry for several days, the water will evaporate, and it will return to its normal volume. You will recover the same amount of Instant Snow powder you started with at the beginning of the experiment.
Scientific Method	Scientific inquiry is a process scientists use to find answers to questions they have about the world around them. They use the steps in the scientific method to design and conduct scientific investigations to explore possible answers. The steps in the scientific method are followed in this experiment.

Related Vocabulary

- **Law of Conservation of Matter**: matter cannot be created or destroyed; it can only change form
- **evaporation**: the process by which liquid water enters the atmosphere as water vapor
- **osmosis**: water molecules pass through a barrier from one side to the other
- **scientific method**: the steps used to design and conduct scientific investigations

Real-World Connection

Many Hollywood movie producers use Instant Snow powder to make realistic snow scenes.

Name: _____ Date: _____

Instant Snow

Purpose: The purpose is a question that asks what you want to learn from the investigation. 1) It should be clearly written, (2) it usually starts with the verb "Does," and (3) it can be answered by measuring something.

Purpose: Does the size of the container affect the rate of water evaporation?

Research: The goal of the research is to find information that will help you make a prediction about what will occur in your experiment. Investigate evaporation and the water cycle. Use the lines below for note taking.

_____

_____

_____

_____

_____

_____

_____

_____

_____

_____

Hypothesis: Make an educated guess about what you think will happen in your project. Your hypothesis should be clearly written. It should answer the question stated in the purpose, be brief and to the point, and identify the independent and dependent variables.

> *Example*: A larger container will (choose one) increase / decrease the
> rate of evaporation.

Hypothesis: _____

_____

_____

_____

Procedure: The procedure is a plan for your experiment. The plan includes a list of the materials needed, step-by-step directions (written like a recipe) for conducting the experiment, and identifies the variables. Measurements are made and recorded using metric units.

Name: _____ Date: _____

Materials Needed:
Instant Snow powder
water
4 different-sized containers made from the same material (plastic, metal, etc.)

Variables: Variables are often referred to as factors, traits, or conditions. The independent variable is the factor that is changed in an experiment. The dependent variable is the factor that responds to the change. The change is measured and recorded in metric units. Write the independent and dependent variables in this experiment below.

Independent: _____

Dependent: _____

Experiment: The experiment is a test designed to answer the question stated in the purpose. The test consists of two groups.

Controlled Setup: The standard or part of the experiment used for comparison.

Step #1: Place the containers on a table in the order from smallest to largest. Number the containers 1 through 4, with the smallest being number 1 and the largest number 4.

Step #2: Place 6 grams (3 teaspoons) of Instant Snow powder in the smallest container.

Step #3: Add 60 mL (2 ounces) of water to the powder to make snow.

Step #4: Place the container in a sunny location in the room.

Step #5: Record the beginning date of the experiment. Check the container daily. Record the date the water was completely evaporated in the data table below. Calculate and record the total number of days it took the water to evaporate.

Experimental Setup: The parts of the experiment that are changed and tested.

Step #1: Repeat steps 2–5 for the other containers.

Results: Record the starting date, ending date, and total number of days in the data table below.

Control Setup			
Container	**Starting Date**	**Ending Date**	**Total Number of Days**
Container #1			
Experimental Setup			
Container	**Starting Date**	**Ending Date**	**Total Number of Days**
Container #2			
Container #3			
Container #4			

Name: _____ Date: _____

Analysis: Study the results of your experiment. Create a bar graph that will compare the data from the control setup with the experimental setup. Place the number of days on the *y*-axis and the number of the container on the *x*-axis.

Container Size and Rate of Evaporation

Number of Days
(y-axis)

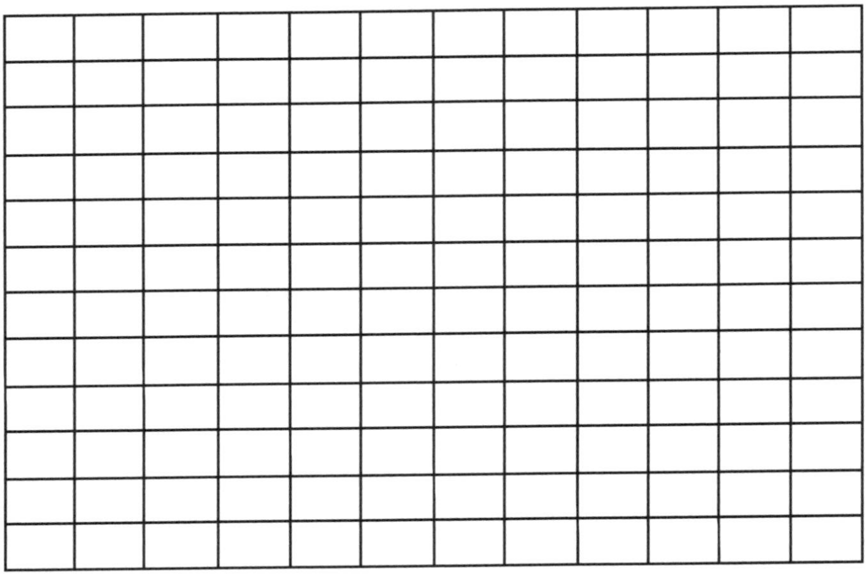

(x-axis)
Containers

Conclusion: Write a summary of the experiment (what actually happened). It should include the purpose, a brief description of the procedure, and whether or not the hypothesis was supported by the data collected. Use key facts from your research to help explain the results. The conclusion should be written in first person ("I").

_____

_____

_____

_____

_____

_____

_____

_____

Name: _____ Date: _____

Ooey Gooey Science Investigation Rubric Scoring Guide

Category	4	3	2	1
Participation	Used time well, cooperative, shared responsibilities, and focused on the task.	Participated, stayed focused on task most of the time.	Participated, but did not appear very interested. Focus was lost on several occasions.	Participation was minimal OR student was unable to focus on the task.
Components of Investigation	All required elements of the investigation were correctly completed and turned in on time.	All required elements were completed and turned in on time.	One required element was missing/or not completed correctly.	The work was turned in late and/or several required elements were missing and/or completed incorrectly.
Procedure	Steps listed in the investigation were accurately followed.	Steps listed in the investigation were followed.	Steps in the investigation were followed with some difficulty.	Unable to follow the steps in the investigation without assistance.
Mechanics	Flawless spelling, punctuation, and capitalization.	Few errors.	Careless or distracting errors.	Many errors.

Comments:

Answer Keys

Hands-On Activities: Answer may vary
Oobleck (page 4)
Observations: When a handful of oobleck is squeezed, it forms a solid. Stop squeezing, and it will run like a liquid.
Conclusion: Oobleck is a non-Newtonian fluid. It has properties of both a solid and a liquid.

Blubber (page 6)
Observations: Playing with the blubber makes it more solid.
Conclusion: Blubber is a non-Newtonian fluid. It has properties of both a solid and a liquid. Non-Newtonian fluids get more solid when they are manipulated. Let blubber sit, and it will ooze like a liquid.

Making Lightning (page 8)
Observations: A small spark occurs when touching the finger to the pie pan.
Conclusion: Lightning happens when the negatively charged electrons in the clouds are attracted to the positively charged protons in the ground. This is similar to the static caused by the charges on the pie plate and finger.

Polymer Bouncing Ball (page 10)
Observations:
1. The borax is a connecting agent that joins the glue and the pudding mix (polymers) together, making the ball bounce.
2. Answers will vary depending on the type of surface on which the ball is bounced.
3. Answers will vary depending on the type of surface on which the ball is bounced.
Conclusion: The bouncing ball is made from a polymer. The long polymer chains can be stretched out or balled up, which makes the material elastic.

Secret Message (page 12)
Observations: The goldenrod indicator paper turns bright red when the baking soda solution is applied. The paper changes back to yellow when the vinegar solution is applied over the baking soda solution base. The opposite happens when applying the vinegar solution and then the baking soda solution.

Conclusion: The goldenrod-colored paper is an acid-base indicator.

Briquette Crystals (page 14)
Observations: Different-colored crystals began to form on the briquettes as the water evaporated.
Conclusion: Crystallization occurs when salt molecules join together as the liquid evaporates into the air. Crystal formations are speeded up by sprinkling salt on the briquettes.

It's in the Bag Ice Cream (page 16)
Observations: The ice cream mixture is a liquid before the crushed ice is added. It becomes a solid after the salted ice freezes it.
Conclusion: The ice absorbs heat energy from the ice cream mixture. The salt lowers the freezing point of the ice. This causes the temperature of the mixture to drop and the cream mixture to freeze.

Teacher Demonstrations
Glowing Pickle (page 18)
Observations: The pickle glowed when the electric current flowed through it.
Conclusion: When energy is added to electrons in an atom, they give off visible light. Add energy in the form of electricity to the sodium atoms in a pickle, and the pickle will glow.

Egg in a Bottle (page 20)
Observations: The egg wobbles as the flame is extinguished.
Conclusion: The fire burns up the oxygen inside the bottle, creating less air pressure. The greater air pressure on the outside of the bottle forces the egg into the bottle.

Things to Make
Bubble Observatory (page 22)
Observations:
1. 7 colors
2. The colors change as the thickness of the bubble layer diminishes.
3. black
Conclusion: Colors come from the light reflected from the soap bubble.

Squawking String (page 24)

Observations:
1. High notes are heard.
2. Low notes are heard.
3. Shortening the string makes the sound higher.

Conclusion: Friction is created as your fingers rub and slide down the string; this causes the string to vibrate. Sound is produced by these vibrations. The cup works likes a speaker, amplifying the sound as the vibrations move up to the cup.

Balloon-Powered Racer (page 26)

Conclusion: The Balloon Racer demonstrates Newton's Third Law of Motion. When the balloon is released, the air is forced through the straw at one end of the racer, and that pushes the racer with equal force in the opposite direction.

Air Cushion Vehicle (page 28)

Conclusion: The air from the Shop Vac creates a very thin layer of air between the hovercraft and the floor. The air serves as an invisible cushion that eliminates almost all friction between the vehicle and the surface.

Electronic Quiz Game (page 30)

Observations: When you select a matched pair on the quiz board, the light bulb lights. When you make the wrong match, the light bulb will not light up.

Conclusion: The light bulb lights up when the circuit is complete.

Squeeze Bottle Rocket Launcher (page 32)

Observations: When you squeeze the bottle launcher, the rocket is launched.

Conclusion: The shape of the wing affects the flight of the straw rocket.

Mousetrap Racer (page 34)

Conclusion: The Mousetrap Racer is a compound machine made up of several simple machines: wheel and axle, lever, and pulley. When the stored energy in the spring of the mousetrap is released, the potential energy is transformed into kinetic energy overcoming inertia and moving the racer forward.

Egg Drop Contraption (page 36)

Observations: Answers will vary.

Conclusion: The keys to the egg's survival are to make the egg's stop not quite as sudden as the outside of the contraption and to distribute the force on the egg evenly over its surface.

Pop Bottle Lava Lamp (page 38)

Observations: The oil floats and the droplets join, making one big blob.

Conclusion: Water is denser (heavier) than oil, which is why the oil floats in the water.

Experiments
Oil Spill Clean-Up (page 44)

Results: Answers will vary.

Conclusion: Answers should discuss how much oil each kind of sorbent absorbed and identify which was the most absorbent.

Gas in a Bag (page 48)

Results: Answers will vary.

Conclusion: Answers should indicate that, no matter what amount of reactants were used, the total mass of the products was equal to the mass of the reactants.

Sunscreen (page 52)

Results: Answers will vary.

Conclusion: Answers should indicate that the higher the SPF, the less the UV beads changed colors.

Instant Snow (page 56)

Results: Answers will vary.

Conclusion: Answers should indicate that the larger the amount of surface area, the faster the rate of evaporation.

Bibliography

Websites

About.com. Chemistry: Fun With Pennies
http://chemistry.about.com/cs/
demonstrations/a/aa022204a.htm

Activity TV: Science Experiments For Kids
http://www.activitytv.com/
science-experiments-for-kids

Educational Innovations
http://www.teachersource.com/

Exploratorium: The Science Explorer
http://www.exploratorium.edu/science_explorer/

Jefferson Lab: Teacher Resources
http://education.jlab.org/indexpages/teachers.
php

Mrs. Stewart's Bluing: All About Bluing
http://www.mrsstewart.com/pages/purpose.htm

PBS: Fetch: Games and Activities
http://pbskids.org/fetch/games/activities.html

Science Buddies: Science Fair Project Ideas
http://www.sciencebuddies.org/
science-fair-projects/project_guide_index.shtml

Science Kids at Home: What is Sound?
<http://www.sciencekidsathome.com/
science_topics/what_is_sound.html>

Steve Spangler Science
http://www.stevespanglerscience.com/

**University Corporation for Atmospheric
Research: Web Weather for Kids**
http://eo.ucar.edu/webweather/index.html

Utah Education Network: Air Has Pressure
<http://www.uen.org/Lessonplan/preview.cgi?
LPid=1686>

**Utah State University Cooperative Extension:
Agriculture in the Classroom**
http://utah.agclassroom.org

Weather Wiz Kids: Weather Experiments
http://www.weatherwizkids.com/
weather-experiments.htm

Books

Beaver, John B. and Don Powers. *Electricity and Magnetism: Static Electricity, Current Electricity, and Magnets.* Quincy, Illinois: Mark Twain Media, Inc., 2010.

Beaver, John B. and Barbara R. Sandall. *Simple Machines: Forces, Motion, and Energy.* Quincy, Illinois: Mark Twain Media, Inc., 2010.

Krebs, Robert, E. *Encyclopedia of Scientific Principles, Laws, and Theories.* Santa Barbara, CA: Greenwood Press. 2008.

Hollihan, Kerrie Logan. *Isaac Newton and Physics for Kids: His Life and Ideas with 21 Activities.* Chicago: Chicago Review Press. 2009.

Jargodzki, Christopher and Franklin Potter. *Mad About Physics: Braintwisters, Paradoxes, and Curiosities.* New York: Wiley. 2000.

Logan, LaVerne. *Geology: Rocks, Minerals, and the Earth.* Quincy, Illinois: Mark Twain Media, Inc., 2010.

Logan, LaVerne and Don Powers. *Meteorology: Atmosphere and Weather.* Quincy, Illinois: Mark Twain Media, Inc., 2010.

Sandall, Barbara R. *Chemistry: Physical and Chemical Changes in Matter.* Quincy, Illinois: Mark Twain Media, Inc., 2010.

Sandall, Barbara R. *Light and Color: Connecting Students to Science Series.* Quincy, Illinois: Mark Twain Media, Inc., 2004.

Sandall, Barbara R., and LaVerne Logan. *Light and Sound: Energy, Waves, and Motion.* Quincy, Illinois: Mark Twain Media, Inc., 2010.

Sciencesaurus: A Student Handbook. Houghton Mifflin, 2002.

Shireman, Myrl. *Physical Science.* Quincy, Illinois: Mark Twain Media, Inc., 1997.

Westphal, Laurie. *Hands-On Physical Science.* Waco, TX: Prufrock Press. 2007.

National Science Standards Matrix

Each unit is designed to strengthen scientific literacy and support the National Science Education Standards (NSES).

Units	Unifying Concepts and Processes	A	B	C	D	E	F	G
Hands-On Activities								
Matter: Oobleck	X	X	X					
Non-Newtonian Fluid: Blubber	X	X	X					
Weather: Making Lightning	X	X			X			
Chemical Change: Polymer Bouncing Ball	X	X	X					
Acids and Bases: Secret Message	X	X	X					
Rocks and Minerals: Briquette Crystals	X	X			X			
Physical Change: It's in the Bag Ice Cream	X	X	X					
Teacher Demonstrations								
Atoms: Glowing Pickle	X	X	X					
Atmospheric Pressure: Bottled Egg	X	X	X					
Things to Make								
Light: Bubble Observatory	X	X	X			X		
Sound: Squawking String	X	X	X			X		
Motion: Balloon-Powered Racer	X	X	X			X		X
Friction: Air Cushion Vehicle	X	X	X			X		
Electricity: Electronic Quiz Game	X	X	X			X		
Bernoulli's Principle: Bottle Rocket Launcher	X	X	X			X		X
Magnetism: Magnetic Soccer Game	X	X	X			X		
Machines: Mousetrap Racer	X	X	X			X		
Gravity: Egg Drop Contraption	X	X	X			X		X
Density: Pop Bottle Lava Lamp	X	X	X			X		
Experiments								
Sorbents: Oil Spill Clean-Up	X	X	X	X		X	X	
Law of Conservation of Matter: Gas in a Bag	X	X	X					
Electromagnetic Spectrum: Sunscreen	X	X	X				X	
Evaporation: Instant Snow	X	X	X					

*For more detailed information on each content standard, go to <www.nap.edu/catalog/4962.html> or see the book *National Science Education Standards* (ISBN 0-309-05326-9).

Ooey Gooey Science Photo Credits

pg. 3 Ketchup with bottle. ©iStockphoto.com/ Gary518.

pg. 4 Disgusted by Science. ©iStockphoto.com/ lisafx.

pg. 6 Slime lila. {{PD-GNU}} Kungfuman.

pg. 8 Homemade Lightning. ©doitscience.com

pg. 9 Colorful Super ball. {{PD-GNU}} Beao.

pg. 10 Bouncy Balls. ©iStockphoto.com/Nicky-Blade.

pg. 11 Mais Direktsaa021. {{PD-CC}} Volker Prasuhn.

pg. 12 Baking Soda & Water. ©Sarah H. Davis. <www.unplugyourkids.com>

pg. 13 Housework. ©iStockphoto.com/tacojim.

pg. 15 Old Ice Cream Maker. ©iStockphoto.com/ DIGIcal.

pg. 15 Gelatiera. {{PD-GNU}} ElinorD.

pg. 17 Feuerwerk Raketen. {{PD-Author}} Jon Sullivan.

pg. 18 Kiszony ogorek. {{PD-CC-BY}} Julienbzh35

pg. 19 Barometer Goethe 02. {{PD-GNU}} Littoclime.

pg. 20 Chicken egg 2009-06-04. {{PD-CC-BY-SA 3.0}} Sun Ladder.

pg. 20 Empty Milk bottle isolated with clipping path. ©iStockphoto.com/melkerw.

pg. 21 Antibubble cluster. {{PD-GNU}} TheAlphaWolf

pg. 23 Carlo-domeniconi photo dj-17062009-103. {{PD-GNU}} Davidjohnberlin.

pg. 24 Cup Phone. ©iStockphoto.com/Devonyu.

pg. 25 *Apollo 15* launch. {{PD-USGOV-NASA}} NASA.

pg. 27 Formel1 hovercraft. {{PD-CC}} Thomas Philipp.

pg. 29 IPad-02. {{PD-CC}} Glenn Fleishman. <www.flickr.com/photos/69628725@N00>

pg. 34 SECME Mousetrap-cars. {{PD-GNU}} WillMcC.

pg. 35 Fragile Box. ©iStockphoto.com/Andrew-Johnson.

pg. 36 Egg drop. ©Z Parker. <www.zparkersblog.blogspot.com/2011_03_01_archive.html.>

pg. 37 Deepwater Horizon oil spill - May 24, 2010. {{PD-USGOV-NASA}} NASA.

pg. 38 Homemade Lava Lamp Observation. ©Oakley Originals. <www.flickr.com/photos/oakleyoriginals/6218545245/in/photostream>

pg. 38 Lava lamp operating. {{PD-Author}} TheMexican.

pg. 40 01DawnIBRRC2010.05.04MG5640.{{PD-CC}} International Bird Rescue Research Center. <www.flickr.com/photos/ibrrc/4609321473/>

pg. 40 Deepwater Horizon oil spill - May 24, 2010 - with locator. {{PD-USGOV-NASA}} NASA.

pg. 42 Cleaning Up Oil Spills. ©Julie. <www.just-playin-around.blogspot.com>

pg. 45 Glow in the Dark. ©iStockphoto.com/ cjscott2.

pg. 49 Group of young swimmers. ©iStockphoto.com/kali9.

pg. 51 Bottles of Sun screen on beach. ©iStockphoto.com/cmannphoto.

pg. 53 Vanha Kirkkopuisto lumisateella. {{PD-GNU}} Lumijaguaari.

pg. 55 Measuring cups of snow and water. ©Melynda Harrison <www.travelingmel.com>